recollections

Sketches of Some Early Australian Bahá'ís

Compiled and Edited by
Merle Olivia Heggie (Née Brooks)

Bahá'í Publications Australia

recollections – Sketches of Some Early Australian Bahá'ís

© Merle Olivia Heggie (Née Brooks)

Copyright © 2009 by the National Spiritual Assembly of the Bahá'ís of Australia Incorporated

All rights reserved

ISBN: 1 876322 46 2

Distributed by :
Bahá'í Distribution Services
P.O. Box 300
Bundoora Vic 3083
Australia
Email: bds@bahai.org.au
www.bahaibooks.com

Cover Design & Book Layout : Massoud Tahzib

FORWARD

This collection of sketches is a portrayal of some early Australian Bahá'ís, descendants of one branch of the Brooks family who settled in the 19th century in South Australia, a British colony newly opened in 1836.

It is a story of search for spiritual values, the truth of religion, of values that would relate to a new age. It is not a saga of great physical heroism, of disasters, crises and epic attainment, destined for publicity in the media but brief portraits of the lives of some individuals who searched, found and accepted the Bahá'í Faith. Their story reveals the power and effect of the Bahá'í Revelation on many individuals, although it may not explain why so many of one family and their descendants accepted Bahá'u'lláh as the Manifestation of God for today.

I have written the sketches simply and without undue detail. Certainly it is not a detailed biography of any of the family. It has been an enjoyable task.

I dedicate these tributes to my Bahá'í ancestors who passed on their knowledge and faith in Bahá'u'lláh to me and gave me their love and support in my early days. It is a small expression of my ever-growing love and appreciation for them. May God bless all our descendants.

Merle Heggie
Sydney 2009

ACKNOWLEDGEMENTS

Valuable help was given by members of this family, viz. my children, Jennifer and her husband David (who scanned the pictures and did the layout) Adrian, Christopher and his wife, Bita (who typed the manuscript and made many valuable suggestions). My sister, Margaret Chittleborough and brother Norman Brooks. Dawn Dibdin, my cousin, contributed the complete sketch of Geoff and herself. Allaine Duncan-Fish and Ruth Park supplied the sketch of Colin Duncan. Thanks are also due to Tom Dowson and Mary Anne Palliaer for their touching anecdotes and to Massoud Tahzib for his encouragement in publishing this book and for the design of the cover and the final layout.

Merle Heggie
Sydney 2009

CONTENTS

SECTION I

First Generation Bahá'ís

1. The Brooks family - one of its branches..................3
2. The very early years of the Bahá'í Faith in Australia............9
3. Some remarkable members of the Brooks family

   - Hilda Margaret Thomas (née Brooks)..........................17
   - Rose Elizabeth Hawthorne (née Brooks)......................21
   - David Arthur Brooks (author's father).........................27
   - Amy Olive Brooks (née Mills) (author's mother).............35
   - Frank Dempster Brooks...37
   - Marjorie Winifred Duncan (née Brooks).......................39
   - Margaret Dempster Brooks (mother of five children who became Bahá'í)..43

SECTION II

Second Generation Bahá'ís

1. Merle Olivia Heggie (née Brooks)..47
2. Margaret Maud Chittleborough (née Brooks).......................59
3. Norman David Brooks...63
4. Colin Duncan..67
5. Dawn Dibdin (née Duncan)...71
6. Jim and Merle participating in the Six Year Plan...................79

CONTENTS
(Continued)

SECTION III

James Heggie

Contents and forward 89

PART 1 : An Autobiography by James Heggie 95

PART 2 : James Heggie's First visit to the Baháʾí World Centre and meeting the Beloved Guardian December 1941 105

PART 3 : James Heggie's Second visit to the Baháʾí World Centre and meeting the Beloved Guardian January 1942 119

PART 4 : Quotes in letters from the Beloved Guardian regarding James Heggie 125

SECTION IV

Some Interesting Photographs 129

The Family Tree 146

Epilogue 150

SECTION ONE

First Generation Bahá'ís

Family group; L-R standing: David Brooks, Hilda Brooks, Marjorie Brooks,
Rose Hawthorne née Brooks and husband William Hawthorne.
Seated: Frank Brooks, Margaret Brooks née Dempster

Norman Leonard Brooks who died in the
First World War, brother of David, Frank,
Hilda, Rose and Marjorie Brooks

recollections   Sketches of Some Early Australian Bahá'ís

THE BROOKS FAMILY

A BRIEF HISTORY OF ONE OF ITS BRANCHES

It seems appropriate to start with Joseph and Elizabeth Brooks, grandparents of the first declarants who, though never hearing of Bahá'í, must have had some influence on their descendants in character, work ethos, pioneering stamina and ethics.

"Joseph and Elizabeth have been described as 'Strict Bible Christians'. The Church known as Bible Christians, was formed in 1815 in North Devon, England, by William O'Bryan as a breakaway from the Wesleyan Methodist Church. It was very evangelical and accepted women into the Ministry equally with men. It later merged into the Methodist Church which in Australia later became part of the Uniting Church. " (1)

Brooks, spelt in a number of variations, is a well-known English surname and according to records was first used as a surname in 1130 A.D. A bearer of the name denoted a dweller near a stream or water-meadow. There have been many families with this name; numerous descendants are scattered around the globe. This account is concerned only with the branch stemming from Joseph and Elizabeth Brooks (née Stokes) who left their home in Worcestershire with two children, sailing as assisted migrants to South Australia leaving Portsmouth on the 26th February 1838 in the "Eden" and arriving after four months - apparently a fast passage at that time because there were no ports of call on the way - and landing at Holdfast Bay (now known as Glenelg) on the 24th of June, only eighteen months after the first arrivals to this new colony.

"The passengers were lowered over the side in baskets and taken ashore with their luggage by the sailors". (2)

Joseph seems to have been a resourceful, hard-working and enterprising

---

Quotes 1 & 2 were from notes by R.A. Brooks from "The Story of a pioneer of South Australia", Joseph Brooks (1815-1860) pp 7 & 5, respectively.

man, making enough money to buy land and cultivate crops with varying success and doing reasonably well at times, in country around Adelaide. He was the developer of the soft-shelled almond according to several of his descendants; nothing came of this achievement perhaps because he died early or for other reasons. Joseph Brooks died in 1860 at the age of forty-six.

Elizabeth re-married a Samuel Francis Smith who has been described as a "ne'er-do-well". She died on the 21st April 1894. There are many other details of these settlers but not of special relevance to this story. What is relevant to this family history is the story of William, the seventh son of Joseph and Elizabeth, who married Margaret Dempster of Scottish ancestry from Tarcowie. This union produced a family of eleven children, five of whom became Bahá'í as did many of their descendants.

A brief sketch of these individuals' lives may give us some understanding of their attraction to the Bahá'í Faith.

The Revelation of Bahá'u'lláh came to Australia in 1920 with the arrival of John Henry and Clara Hyde-Dunn from U.S.A. Their enthusiasm, sincerity and dedication to the Teachings of Bahá'u'lláh resulted in the establishment of the Bahá'í Faith in Sydney, Melbourne and Adelaide in the early 1920's and these two elderly people were held in high regard by the many Australians they met, becoming affectionately known as "Mother" and "Father" Dunn.

A notable Bahá'í visitor to Australia in 1931/32 was an American woman, Mrs. Keith Ransome-Kehler who arrived by ship after weeks of travel with many necessary trunks of clothing and books for such a project as teaching the Bahá'í Faith by lectures, informal talks and introductions to people of standing or influence in this society. I have always understood Keith to have been a gifted speaker and lecturer. Certainly she aroused deep interest in several members of the Brooks family who attended her talks in Adelaide, South Australia at that time. I understand it was an early believer in Adelaide, a Mrs. Truman, who suggested that Hilda Brooks, Rose Hawthorne (her sister) and Will Hawthorne, (Rose's husband) attend her lectures. Probably these people met at other lectures or similar gatherings in their search for new ideas and answers to questions. Now, decades later, we have the powerful medium of television to influence and educate people. The wireless in those days was being well-established, filling a vacuum in communication, education and entertainment.

The capital cities had a few major newspapers in which some overseas news appeared usually about politics, wars, catastrophes, various or outlandish happenings and to be fair some erudite articles. But, people did go to public lectures and among the venues offered to Bahá'í travelling teachers were the "New Thought" and "Theosophical" platforms on several of which Keith spoke. And so among her audience were Miss Hilda Brooks, Mrs. Rose (née Brooks) Hawthorne and Mr. William Hawthorne. It was not long before they became members of the small Adelaide Bahá'í group that became a Local Spiritual Assembly possibly in the later 1920's; nor did Hilda hesitate to inform her brother David about this Revelation.

The parents of these early Bahá'ís were William and Margaret Brooks who had settled on land in the lower Flinders district which had first to be cleared of mallee and cultivated to produce crops, mostly wheat and grasses for pasture. From this perspective, life must have been hard and demanding; the British colony not yet a century old. Horses were the essential beasts of burden, toil and the means of travel until machines, tractors, motorcars and trucks appeared and relieved men of the old hardships. Essential services such as shops, schools, post offices, hospitals, institutes, libraries etcetera gradually became a part of the life of the inhabitants of South Australia; roads and rail tracks were laid down, bringing people in closer contact to Adelaide which was growing into a city.

Women worked hard too, but there was an active social life in the country providing pleasures of sport, dancing, concerts and singing around the piano, recitations, storytelling and sharing jokes. Friendships were formed. On the intellectual level the offering at first must have been limited. Primary schools were quickly established; children walked or rode a horse or bicycle to their nearest village or town school. High schools were opened and some young people would go on to Adelaide to further their education or qualify as an artisan. The churches of the district were well attended.

William and Margaret were very devoted Methodists. A lasting tribute to William Brooks, in the form of a stained-glass window in the local church, can still be seen. William served as a lay preacher for some time with the church. I understand they read from the Bible to the family on a regular basis, probably weekly possibly daily and their nine children with them attended Sunday church. Marjorie Duncan (née Brooks), William's youngest child remembers her father often quoting "for the earth shall be filled with the knowledge of the glory of the Lord, as the waters cover the sea" (Habakkuk 2.14), thus testifying his faith in the Holy Scriptures and belief in the future of mankind.

Margaret Dempster (née Brooks) and William Brooks

Nevertheless a precursor of future revolt was gradually stirring some family members in a mild way. It was an old custom on Sundays to have a hot mid-day dinner with family and sometimes friends. Thus two members had to miss church and prepare this meal. The church was six miles away and transport then was by horse and trap, meaning an absence of about three hours for the church attendants. Rose, a young teenager and Hilda still a youngster, would plead to stay at home, ostensibly making a spiritual sacrifice, but as Rose explained they were beginning to tire of church doctrine and years later as young women, they were immediately attracted to the Bahá'í Faith when they heard Keith Ransom-Kehler's discourse on Bahá'í principles. On investigating the Faith many questions were answered and a new horizon opened up.

HAND OF THE CAUSE OF GOD
KEITH RANSOM-KEHLER

Keith Ransom-Kehler Hand of the Cause and the first American Martyr

Keith Ransom-Kehler, was born 14th February 1876, a native of Dayton, Kentucky, became a Bahá'í in May 1921 some ten years after meeting 'Abdu'l-Bahá in London. Keith was an accomplished academic and a gifted public speaker. On one occasion in New York she gave a series of talks to audiences of up to 500, and at the final gathering she asked that only those who considered themselves to be Bahá'í stay. The result was thirty five new Bahá'ís. In recognition of this Shoghi Effendi sent thirty five Bahá'í ring stones as gifts.

In February 1929 having lost her husband to illness, Keith embarked on a world tour, directed by the Beloved Guardian, Shoghi Effendi to spread the Teachings to the Caribbean, parts of South America, Japan, China, Australia, New Zealand and India. During her visit to Australia she gave talks in Brisbane, Newcastle, Sydney, Melbourne and Adelaide these last being attended by Hilda and Rose Brooks who shared their new knowledge with the rest of the Brooks family.

With thoughts of wonder and humility members of my family feel a special gratitude and love for Keith as we contemplate her influence in bringing us the Revelation of Bahá'u'lláh.

Keith became the first American Bahá'í martyr after travelling to Iran as instructed by the Guardian.

The Guardian's secretary wrote: "She rendered wonderful services in both Australia and India."

On 30th October 1933 the Guardian sent the following message to the Bahá'í World :

> "Keith's precious life offered up in sacrifice to beloved Cause in Bahá'u'lláh's native land."

For further information on the life of Keith Ransom-Kehler, see *"The Bahá'í World 1932-1934"* and also *"A Love Which Does Not Wait"* by Janet Ruhe-Schoen.

recollections   Sketches of Some Early Australian Bahá'ís

EARLY YEARS

As I look back at my early years I marvel at the gradual development of this Faith here in Australia since Mother and Father Dunn came to these shores in 1920. On becoming a Bahá'í youth in my early teens at my home in a country district I couldn't have realized what a tremendous step I had taken. However, it didn't stop me from launching into teaching for I almost immediately told my best friend, Dorothy Sanders, about Bahá'u'lláh's Teachings. We rode on our horses at weekends to visit each other at our respective home farms in the Lower Flinders region and shared interests. I recall the confidence I felt that Dorothy would naturally accept the logic of progressive religion. But Dorothy kept her belief in 'only Christianity' and over the years has worked in the Uniting Church. She really is to this day a perfect model of all she believes in and is highly thought of in the community.

As a youth of seventeen years old, I went to Adelaide in 1937 to continue my education. There were perhaps about thirty believers who met regularly in a rented room in Epworth Building, Adelaide City, for Feasts and a monthly public lecture. Apart from my relatives some of those very early believers included Mrs. Maisie Almond, Mrs. Trueman, Mrs. Silver Jackman, Mr. Robert Brown, Mr. Harold and Mrs. Florence Fitzner, Mrs. Bertha and Mr. Joe Dobbins, Miss Dorothy Douglas, Miss Leila Clark, Mr. and Mrs. Appleton, Mrs. Johnson, Mr. and Mrs. Allen, Mrs. Beaumont, Lucy Trueman (youth) and also a few children. Some of these were members of the N.S.A. and L.S.A. and some of them pioneered overseas years later.

I lived for about two years with my Aunt Rose and Uncle Will Hawthorne in Millswood suburb and very soon Aunt Rose established a monthly, youth fireside to which I would invite my friends and acquaintances whom I met at Adelaide University, the Conservatorium of Music and the School of Arts. Introducing the Faith to those of my own age seemed quite easy, perhaps because there were not so many divisions of Christianity and a plethora of new movements as appeared in later years. Many came to those firesides and enjoyed themselves. Aunt Rose was a charming hostess, had a comfortable home and supplied a delicious supper after an explanation of the Bahá'í Faith by my other Aunt, Hilda Brooks. There was always discussion at these enjoyable and relaxed evenings.

One of my special friends was a talented pianist who also was a pupil, like myself, of William Silver at the Conservatorium. Ronda Gehling, of German parents, came from the Barossa Valley and had attended the Lutheran Church until she came to Adelaide, there becoming a Church of England member. It upset her when I explained the principle of progressive Revelation and particularly the station of Muhammad. I then learnt that it was necessary to be aware of a person's feelings and outlook and not rush in where angels fear to tread. It saddened me to see Ronda weep, in fact it was a shock to me. Later I read where a Lutheran minister preached in church against Muhammad, so possibly Ronda had already been prejudiced while still a Lutheran.

I hadn't then followed 'Abdu'l-Bahá's ways and example. In fact in those days I hadn't studied the Writings. Only a few books were available to me and I certainly had little money to spend on them. While still at home my father had given me a prayer book and he persuaded me to read *"Security for a Failing World"* by Stanwood Cobb and *"Bahá'u'lláh and the New Era"* by J.E. Esselmont, the latter at the time becoming my standard reference. My father also had been lent the old edition, *"Bahá'í Scriptures"*, which I probably perused.

Later, in Adelaide, when seventeen or eighteen years of age, I obtained copies of other books such as *"The Hidden Words"* (Pub. in 1920), *"Gleanings from the Writings of Bahá'u'lláh"* (1939), also, though not in this order: "Paris Talks" (then published as *"The Wisdom of 'Abdu'l-Bahá"*), *"Prayers and Meditations"* and *"Some Answered Questions"*. Shoghi Effendi was in touch with the Bahá'í world through his inspiring letters, cables, messages and such publications as *"The Advent of Divine Justice"*, and *"'The Promised Day is Come"* published with other articles in *"The World Order of Bahá'u'lláh"* (1938). *"God Passes By"* came to us in 1944 in time for the centenary of The Báb's Declaration. Copies were then presented to clergy. And now what an abundance of Bahá'í literature we have compared with those early years.

After graduating and having a teaching job in Kapunda, South Australia, in 1943 I arranged with my Uncle Will Hawthorne to purchase on credit a supply of Bahá'í books. He was librarian and agent for the imported books coming from Great Britain and the U.S.A. For a time, while librarian, his bookcase and storage of new copies were in Aunt Rose's dining room and a magnet for me when I visited Aunt and Uncle from the country at weekends.

The word "deepening" wasn't a word I recall being used in my youth. Members of my family urged me to study and teach, both of which I enjoyed. The word "deepening" has a much wider and more significant meaning than "study": like the ocean it can provide a wealth of food and experience, but in spiritual realms. We learnt much from the readings at Feasts and Holy Days. I had occasionally to give a talk on some aspect of the Faith thus forcing me to delve into the Writings. In term vacations spent at *Rockwood*, my father and I had wonderful discussions. I well remember the occasion when I was encouraged to do the Fast. My aunts were determined I would become a knowledgeable, capable Bahá'í. This was all a part of my "deepening".

I do welcome and admire the efforts offered by communities now to educate the children, youth and adults in various aspects of the Faith. How casual my early years appear to me, yet there is a sweet remembrance of sharing love and knowledge with those precious friends.

After World War II came to an end in 1946 with the nuclear explosion, Australians were unsettled, hopeful of world peace but not confident of a wonderful future. Soldiers were being discharged and others were freed from the war conditions. Jobs and homes had to be found. Very little building had taken place for years. Re-adapting to civilian life was sometimes traumatic for army personnel. At least the Bahá'ís had faith in the future, well maybe the distant future, nevertheless we were working towards peace, justice and unity. We always had Shoghi Effendi's guidance. My future husband James Heggie had the very great privilege of meeting Shoghi Effendi during his stay in Palestine as a soldier. This story is told later on in this book.

James Heggie was elected to the National Spiritual Assembly of the Bahá'ís of Australia and as national secretary just before we married in 1947. After the formation of the National Spiritual Assembly of Australia and New Zealand in 1934, isolated believers appeared miraculously it seemed in country areas, in small and large towns and cities. In 1944, the N.S.A. bought a two-storey building, a private home, in Centennial Park, Sydney, opposite the beautiful park. NSA members had searched for a suitable headquarters and I know my Aunt Hilda was involved but I think Mrs. Axford of New Zealand played a large part in this project, also Sydney members. I never met Mrs. Axford but regard her as one of the early stalwarts, serving on the N.S.A. and travel teaching.

Jim and I lived here about a year when he was N.S.A. secretary. I enjoyed being hostess: involved in meeting enquirers, attending to meals for N.S.A. members, preparing the place for Feasts and lectures and also gardening. It was a central meeting place, very handy for Sydney people at the time. I recall the pleasure mingled with some nervousness on answering the doorbell and opening to visitors, often Bahá'ís but also strangers seeking information about the Faith. One disadvantage of its location was the noise generated by traffic as it was situated on a corner where, nearby, five roads converged. Horns, screaming brakes and crashes were unnerving so we sometimes repaired to the peace in the depths of the large Centennial Park.

The Acquisition of a national headquarters was a great milestone in our short history. We were filled with hope, joy, enthusiasm and confidence in future growth. Always there were messages as beacons of light from the Guardian that inspired and enlightened us.

Over succeeding years many Assemblies were formed, conferences held and new committees appointed. In 1948 Jim and I went to Brisbane in response to the Guardian's Six Year Plan for Australia in which he required Assemblies to be formed in those state capitals still without Assembly status.

Then in the 1950's came a tremendous challenge. Shoghi Effendi instructed the National Spiritual Assembly to build a Mashriqu'l-Adhkár on the land previously acquired for this purpose. It was a major responsibility for all concerned. We were at first amazed; it was hardly believable, but how exciting and encouraged we were and honoured to be allocated this project by the Guardian. Once the foundations were begun, many of the Sydney friends would visit the site at weekends, have picnics there and talk to people curious as to what was going on in this "out-of-the-way" venue in the bush, almost in wilderness. The suburb of St. Ives was still a small village on Sydney's outskirts; nearby suburbs were small "towns" and the road to the Temple site just one lane, to and from the beaches and very congested in summer months, carrying ever-increasing traffic.

"Why ever are you building in this out-of-the-way place?" some visitors asked us. I even heard it referred to as a "God-forsaken-place". Once, a driver of a coach, filled with Bahá'ís attending a conference or convention, became lost. I think it was the occasion of the laying of the foundation, such a special occasion; but the coach arrived just in time for the ceremony. We had lots of fun, although N.S.A. members and the associated committees shouldered much responsibility and time-consuming work. Jim was very much involved, dedicated to the task as were so many friends, but so few compared with our numbers today. Articles have been written about this project. However, small incidents and many experiences have not been recorded. The area was a show place in spring with lovely wild flowers in bloom. Waratahs grew abundantly, looking like climbing red roses from the road in a passing car. A visitor at the opening ceremony was observed from the gallery picking a large armful of waratahs.

Another time, during a working bee, my young daughter, Jennifer, saw a large black snake slithering up the main path to the Temple, no doubt intending to settle in the basement, where there were frogs. Jim was first on the scene. He picked up the mat at the Temple door and threw it at the snake, which was approaching the steps. Someone else had gone for a spade to kill it. By the time they got there the snake was on its way towards the temple basement again. Alas! it had to be quickly killed. This site is now accepted as a flora and fauna sanctuary.

The friends worked very hard preparing for the Dedication of the Temple in September, 1961, by Amat'u'l-Bahá Rúhíyyih Khánum.

A committee had been appointed to prepare readings and supervise every Sunday service following dedication. Those involved with this task were Thelma Perks, Bessie Walker, Greta Lake, Nell McMiles and myself, as well as others over the years. We contemplated this task, before and after the dedication with trepidation. How could we cope with this on-going, weekly assignment, presenting a service for the public? It was constant and demanding but we enjoyed it despite our anxieties. Suitable readings had to be selected, readers chosen, usually by telephone, flowers arranged and the Temple cleaning seen to on a regular basis. The N.S.A. formed a number of committees, having to draw from the few believers, possibly 100 or less, at that time. Maintenance, Guiding and Service Committee members usually phoned friends for commitments to serve at the Temple on specific days. Many friends had to be picked up by car, there being no public transport available to the site.

In time I had the pleasure and responsibility of forming and conducting an a cappella choir. This account is told in a separate article. Our first practice is memorable, being held in an old building, long gone I think, in College Street, during a Convention. We trundled up narrow, rather dark stairways to the seclusion of a small room to practice songs arranged with simple harmonies to Bahá'í words by Dorothy Stoney, a Bahá'í of Mudgee. We duly discovered other songs and must attribute our gratitude to MaryAnn McLeod (née Chance) for harmonizing "Yá-Bahá'u'l'Abhá", the melody being by Saffa Kinney and still being sung in the Temple.

The following nine years we found various venues for practice, of necessity being suitable for meeting at night time: viz, at 20 Milling Street, Hunter's Hill (my home), the National Headquarters at Centennial Park, a home in Cook Road, also a singer's studio in the city, with a rehearsal in the Temple. All this seems a long time ago, being in the 1960's and 1970's. The choir is well established and now sings at every service.

Over the years devoted believers with whom I worked on committees became close and very dear friends including Thelma Perks (a Counsellor for some years) Greta and Aubrey Lake, Jean Hutchinson-Smith and daughter Alicia, Jane Routh, Nell McMiles, Noel and Bessie Walker, Ruth Sale and many others. These friends, have passed on to the Abhá Kingdom. There are many others.

On arriving in Sydney in 1947 after our marriage in Adelaide and honeymoon in Melbourne, where we met the friends and I particularly remember Emily and Cyril Easey, Jim and I were welcomed by the community with a celebration party at headquarters, 2 Lang Road, Paddington. The Walker family (Noel and Bessie), Gladys Moody, Charlotte Moffit (known as "Moff'), Jane Routh and those mentioned above were loving hosts to us in their homes and we were settled into our new responsibilities.

Attending the Yerrinbool Bahá'í School became a significant part of life, offering so much to improve our knowledge, our deepening and providing companionship. This was especially so as our children grew, learnt and participated.

Apart from Bahá'í activities there were many other interests. In later years Thelma and I enjoyed attending opera, concerts and ballet performances. I took my children to Bahá'í gatherings, occasionally leaving them with a baby-sitter. During one period, while living in Penshurst, I would drive to

Caringbah where luncheon meetings were held by the friends in the small Bahá'í hall. My youngest child at the time was Adrian, aged about three; he played happily with their box of toys during talks and discussion. Maybe ten to twenty people, including some visitors, would be present. Greta Lake, Nell McMiles and others were responsible for organizing these memorable occasions. This Centre is now a most attractive Bahá'í Centre for the district of Sutherland.

I think the old cliché that human nature never changes is nonsense. This planet is subject to constant change and people, individually and collectively, change. The light from the Manifestations of God brings about mankind's progress and civilizations are established. Looking back over sixty years or more there has been constant growth and change.

Our Bahá'í priorities have been teaching and establishing the administration. In my early years as a Bahá'í the response from a person to the Teachings was often curiosity or a request for information. Nowadays, the response can be, "Not another religion!", sometimes a general and even enthusiastic agreement, or an answer that blocks any further discussion. This latter response comes from individuals rigidly adhering to their old beliefs. The principles of the Faith used to impress, but not now as many of the Teachings of Bahá'u'lláh, once new, even revolutionary, are largely and widely accepted, if not practiced. A multitude of new movements and religious sects have arisen. The knowledge available about almost any subject seems prolific. Materialism overwhelms us at least in the west. The existence of God or a Creator is no longer the basis of many beliefs. Yet it is obvious that many people are looking or wanting spiritual experiences and values. Thus teaching the Faith is a great privilege, joy and challenge and the Faith continues to make tremendous advances in the world.

I know it is easy to make generalizations and yet we can find some truth in them. This is an attempt to mention in brief the differences I have found in teaching and serving the Faith through the years.

Hilda Margaret Thomas (née Brooks)

Some remarkable members of the Brooks family

Hilda Margaret Thomas (née Brooks)
14/7/1896 - 13/1/1969

Hilda was born in 1896, July 14th, the fifth child of Margaret and William, grew up on her parents' property, later named *Rockwood* and attended a school at Arwakurra, a small village at the time, but now disappeared. On the death of her father, William, her brothers took over management of the farm and Hilda, Marjorie (her younger sister) and mother went to Adelaide to live at 17 Gurney Road, Rosepark in an attractive bungalow with a large suburban garden of fruit trees and flowers. Here she was free to pursue in a wider field her investigation into new avenues of thought. As already noted she discovered the new Revelation and embraced it, becoming a member in 1931 or 1932. She said that one of the Bahá'í principles that appealed at first was "the equality of men and women", a really new concept in those days. From that time, then in her mid-thirties, Hilda lived and worked for the Faith, either teaching her friends or acquaintances, giving lectures, writing articles and becoming involved in administration almost until the time of her passing on 13 January, 1969. She had a keen, analytical mind, a good, in fact excellent memory, a sense of humour and she loved to laugh and socialize.

In her youthful days she had been engaged to someone whom I understand was a racehorse owner from Western Australia. The engagement was broken. I never heard of any heartbreak there. Later in 1946 she married Ewart Thomas, one of the devoted early Bahá'ís of Adelaide, who had become a member about the same time as Hilda. Ewart, a World War I veteran and suffering ill health in consequence, died in 1977.

Hilda enjoyed music and must have learnt to play the violin. Unfortunately I didn't hear her play; she never referred to it in my hearing, otherwise, I would have enquired about her interest. As a young child, in the mid 1920's I spent a few holidays with Hilda and my Grandma. Hilda was a very loving Aunt, teasing, cuddling, praising and talking to me I well remember. This was long before she heard of the Faith. However, I recall she didn't attend church while I was there - had she already given up going, I wonder.

Hilda Margaret Brooks

Hilda was a member of the Adelaide Bahá'í Assembly for many years, and later of Burnside. When the National Spiritual Assembly of Australia and New Zealand was formed in 1934 she was elected and made secretary, much to her amazement and dismay really, because she considered herself unqualified and even needing to learn to type.

When she first took on the secretariat of both the Adelaide and National Assemblies (when formed) I was still living in the country at *Rockwood*, so I am not aware of how she set about preparing herself, viz.: to learn about the Faith, particularly the Administration, the working of committees and Assemblies, learning to type and settling down to such responsibilities, but she certainly did arise to the occasion. She had a great sense of responsibility and by the time I went to live in Adelaide in 1937, serving the Faith had become the focus of her life, her joy and inspiration. Fortunately she didn't have to earn a living, receiving financial support from the family property, managed by David Brooks.

Hilda was always conscientious in her work, able to face up to problems and help solve them, very direct in expressing an opinion, perhaps sometimes disconcertingly so. I have always thought of her as being a "tower of strength".

The establishment of the Bahá'í Administration, following Bahá'í procedure and working with other Bahá'ís, all young in the Faith like Hilda, but all coming from the "old world order" with its inadequate practices and attitudes presented a tremendous challenge and no doubt problems for her as an individual and as a member of this new Divine Revelation. One cannot gloss over the stress and worry arising from personality clashes and differences of opinion. Hilda suffered accordingly as part of this scene. Nevertheless those early, devoted, strong characters of that period overcame their problems and differences, followed the Guardian's instructions and served the Faith with loyalty and devotion.

Hilda courageously championed the Faith. She very capably and with courtesy wrote letters refuting the charges or attacks by eminent clergymen (Catholic and Protestant) several times. This correspondence appeared in regional newspapers.

>(For more detail on this, see Dr. Graham Hassall's article "*Women in an Advancing Civilisation. Hilda Brooks and the Australian Bahá'í Community*".)

Mr. Tom Dowson who also served on the N.S.A. during its early years writes of Hilda as follows:

"Arriving in Adelaide in 1933, I met Robert Brown who was expecting me with his genial smile. We were friends at once. "You must meet Hilda Brooks", he said and on Saturday afternoon he took me to Gurney Road. Hilda, I found, was modest, earnest and very well read in Bahá'í Scriptures, was a serious but warm and friendly person. She had firm views, but was not rigid in any way. On the contrary, she was most accommodating of other people's ideas, very patient with difficult enquirers."

"I spent many times with Robert at Gurney Road when Hilda had visitors, and it was a pleasure to see her gently and expertly presenting discussion about the Faith. These qualities were prominent when delivering her many public talks. As an example of her gentle but positive manner, I once remarked in discussion, that society needed more tolerance. Hilda with a firm manner but friendly smile said: 'It's love that is needed, not just tolerance which is simply passive'."

After being relieved of her many years on the N.S.A., Hilda seemed to me to develop a more relaxed personality. She was always a loving aunt - she gave me much help, advice, encouragement and occasionally took me to task especially when I was reluctant to give talks. She had a deep love for the Brooks family, was a great friend and admirer of Jim Heggie. Although I didn't see so much of her after my marriage as we then lived in different cities, I think her latter years away from so much responsibility allowed her to express more openly her love, sympathy and appreciation for people. When on my last visit to her, she welcomed me at the door and I was overwhelmed by her love and joy that flowed from her inmost being.

Finally and of great significance, over the years as N.S.A. secretary, Hilda had been in frequent contact with Shoghi Effendi, either through cables or letters, and through his guidance, she was loyally and diligently trying to establish the Administration for the New World Order in Australia.

I realize that I cannot adequately express the regard and reverence developed and felt by, and apparent in Hilda, for the Guardian of the Cause of Bahá'u'lláh.

Hilda passed on to the Abhá Kingdom on 13th January, 1969 . Her grave is in the Centennial Park Cemetery, Adelaide.

Rose Elizabeth Hawthorne (née Brooks)
1/8/1882 - 7/7/1988

Rose was the second child of William and Margaret, born on August 1st 1882. Twins were the first-born, but did not survive their first two years. The first surviving child was Albert William Brooks, born June 24th, 1880. Being young and enterprising he went to Western Australia where he established a branch of the family. However, he did not become a Bahá'í so he doesn't form part of this 'story'.

At this point I must mention that the fourth son - the sixth child, born on 19th May, 1891, was Norman Leonard who joined the Armed Forces in 1914 and was killed in France in World War I on 11th June, 1917. His death was much mourned by the family. He seemed to be a favourite especially with his sisters and I am mentioning this because Hilda once said to me that he, in the next world, could well have lead them to the Faith. Though who can say how the "breaths and the gentle winds of the Dawn" of this Revelation come to enlighten us? It seems a mysterious bounty and may eternally remain so.

My account of Rose must be rather personal as I was fortunate to live with her and Uncle Will in my early teens in their home at 2 Regent Street, Millswood, an Adelaide suburb, after they had retired from their farm on Eyre Peninsula (S.A.). Rose had married Will Hawthorne on 22 March, 1911 and they lived on a farm in the upper Flinders district before buying land on Eyre Peninsula near Yaninee. Rose must have been a very attractive, lively and intelligent youth, growing into a slim, elegant woman, beautifully dressed with good taste, and in moderation. She was a gracious hostess, welcoming friends and acquaintances with a natural manner and warmth.

Before she discovered the Bahá'í Faith and accepting it at the same time as her sister, Hilda, in 1932, I gather she had attended a range of social functions and concerts in Adelaide. I'm sure she must have heard Gala Curci and other famous artists of the time, and bought their records. I listened to them being played on her gramophone but by the time I lived in her home she and Will were occupied with Bahá'í matters and no longer attended concerts and rarely social functions; playing bridge was no longer an attraction.

I was surprised at the time that neither she nor Will made an overseas trip to Europe, but that was still a long sea voyage. Rose, however, was concerned about health and attended lectures by an American woman, called Phoebe. Alas! I do not remember her full name nor that of her lecture series but it was quite advanced for the time and not upheld by the medical profession. I recall that Phoebe advocated the use of wholemeal flour, wholemeal bread, vegetables, only steamed, plenty of fruit and almost no milk on becoming an adult. This latter 'prohibition' I didn't like as milk-bars were opening up all over the city and country and I had found milk-shakes delicious and they were much imbibed by the young, so milk-bars were crowded with young people. The age of the 'bobby-soxer' had arrived.

Rose, on becoming a Bahá'í, was an active teacher, never reticent but considerate of her listeners and was quite wise. When I lived with her, she held many monthly firesides, as well as separate monthly ones just for the youth.

She made friends easily, and they were happy to visit her on many occasions for she had an attractive home, but I think an added draw-card was her elegant, gracious and welcoming personality. Her firesides were well attended and usually Hilda gave the introductory talk. Neighbours nearby and further along the suburban streets were told of the Faith. On going to her city bank on business she would usually leave a pamphlet with the teller. On becoming an elderly customer she would be escorted out of the bank to her taxi, a pleasant gesture for a lady even in that age.

In their marriage Rose and Will always appeared to be a support for each other and this was especially apparent in their Bahá'í activities. Will was capable and dependable, an intelligent farmer and a devoted and active Bahá'í. He passed away on 27th July, 1947.

Rose and Will served on the Adelaide Spiritual Assembly and then, later on the Unley Spiritual Assembly. Will took on the buying and selling of Bahá'í books for the community. More books were becoming available. He kept them in a bookcase in their dining room.

Rose worked hard advertising the Faith in their area and went travel teaching, regularly, I remember, to Clare, a country town north of Adelaide, and she wasn't young at the time.

One of the many pleasures Rose enjoyed during her teaching trips to Clare was her meeting with the editor of a local newspaper and his response and interest in the Bahá'í Faith. Such was his appreciation that he inserted in his weekly paper a lengthy quote from Writings on the Teachings. This aroused considerable opposition in the district and some readers cancelled their subscriptions to his paper, but this had no effect on the editor's support for Rose. He didn't acknowledge his acceptance of the Faith by joining but the friends agreed that he had a reward in winning first prize in a very large lottery.

Earlier, when Hand of the Cause, Martha Root, visited Adelaide in 1939, Will was a great help accompanied by Rose and Hilda, driving Martha to meetings, lectures and interviews in their comfortable car, a De Soto (which was rather special at the time) and then on to Melbourne to help Martha fulfill her busy schedule of teaching and lectures, and not stopping there, but then on to Tasmania. What a teaching trip for those early days.

Rose and Hilda

Think of the organization required; the friends in Melbourne and Hobart would have worked for many weeks towards arranging for platforms, for interviews, for publicity and the spiritual joy of meeting Hand of the Cause Martha Root. The N.S.A. members and Hilda, as National Secretary, would have had much to do in the arrangements and its success. Rose would have been very attentive to Martha's comfort as she was then frail and not well and Will would have seen to the needs of the car. I remember Rose telling me of their wonderful experiences. Why didn't I record it at the time! The memory can let one down after many years.

Rose lived to be one hundred and five years old, spending her later years in a private nursing home. She became very frail but never stopped teaching the Faith when possible, always attracting publicity and being visited by friends and relatives.

When Rose turned 100, in 1981, Hunter's Hill Bahá'í community in NSW placed the following press release in the local paper, *"The Weekly Times" (TWT)*. It read as follows:

"BAHÁ'Í - ONE HUNDRED YEARS OLD

Mrs. Rose Hawthorne the Aunt of Mrs. Merle Heggie, a Bahá'í resident in Hunter's Hill, turns 100 years old this month. She has been a member of the Bahá'í Faith for 50 years.

Besides the honour of receiving a telegram from the Queen, she was further delighted to receive a visit from the Premier of South Australia, Mr. Tonkin, who presented her with a bouquet of flowers, and to appear on Adelaide's Channel 10 News Service, Friday 30th July, when she spoke briefly on her longevity. Her photo and an article about her appeared in the South Australian morning paper, "The Advertiser" on the same day. She was given two parties by friends and relatives."

An article in the Adelaide Daily Newspaper, The Advertiser, appeared in August 1987, extracts are below:

As a young girl, Rose Hawthorne once walked through Booleroo Centre in SA's Mid North wearing a skirt which revealed a slim ankle.

The elders of the town were astonished at her display and ordered her to get off the street and have her hem adjusted.

Rose Hawthorne turns 105 today but many of her memories of younger days remain vivid.

She cannot remember exactly when it was that she dismayed the country town. Instead, she says it was "too long ago".

Mrs. Hawthorne's eyes widened often yesterday as she recalled - surrounded by flowers, cards and well-wishers at the Victoria Park Nursing Home - some of the more mischievous antics in her life.

Like the day when her parents were not at home and she asked the household maid to cut off her long hair.

"My mother didn't sleep for a week afterwards," she said.

Although a little perturbed that visitors had arrived just when she was having her lunch, it did not take much prompting to get Mrs. Hawthorne to recall her girlhood.

But she said politely" :In the next 100 years you just come when I'm not having dinner.'

She paused to gather her thoughts and then started on another tale about sugar beer her mother used to make for the workers on the family station near Booleroo Centre.

Mrs. Hawthorne, who has outlived her husband, attributes her longevity to *the fact that there's no room "up there" or "down there". She has practised the Bahá'í Faith since 1931.*

The second of ten children, Mrs. Hawthorne has lived at the nursing home for twelve years. Her one surviving sister, now in her 80s, lives in Sydney.

Extracts from the eulogy delivered by her niece, Mrs. Dawn Dibdin:

Rose described her life as a child as full of hard work. She helped bring up the seven children younger than herself. There was no electricity in those days, and water had not been connected to the property. Her mother, Margaret Brooks, even made the candles and soap that the family used.

Rose talked of walking three miles to school every day, and of being so tired after school sometimes she would lie down in a paddock and sleep on her way home. Rose said she was not one of the clever students but she proved to be an excellent seamstress and wonderful cook.

Rose admired the suffragettes and would have joined them, surely, if she had had the opportunity. She bitterly resented the way the men of the family seemed to think the women inferior and thought they were not as bright as themselves. Later when they became Bahá'ís and understood the principle of the "equality of men and women" they laughed about those "bad old days".

Until the day she died, Rose thought of nothing but the Bahá'í Teachings and of ways and means of introducing the Faith to others. She held firesides in her home, where people would come and hear of the Message. For many years she would travel once a month up to Clare, staying in a hotel, and arrange meetings there so people could hear about the Faith. The editor of the local paper became a great friend and agreed to publish in instalments, the book by George Townsend *"Christ and Bahá'u'lláh"*. He received a great deal of criticism for this, but because of his great respect and admiration for Rose, he was not deterred.

Rose passed away on 7th of July, 1988. Her grave is in Centennial Park Cemetery, Adelaide. I imagine her and Hilda in the Abhá Kingdom consulting and arranging ways of serving in the spiritual realms, or reminiscing and laughing over their earthly experiences and they would share their love for Bahá'u'lláh with so many of the early believers.

recollections Sketches of Some Early Australian Bahá'ís

David Arthur Brooks
13/8/1884 - 9/8/1967

My father, David Brooks was the second son of William and Margaret, born on the 13th of August, 1884 and became a Bahá'í in his 40s in either 1932 or 33. He was an isolated believer, living in a very conservative, rural district of Christians, of various sects such as Roman Catholic, Lutheran, Methodist and Church of England, most of whose members in those days regularly attended church and were intolerant of other sects, and they discouraged inter-marriage or attending other churches than their own.

Now, a century later, much of that intolerance is disappearing and the community seems to be growing into a stage of ecumenical harmony. The new ideas and principles laid down by Bahá'u'lláh have surely seeped into people's hearts and minds. Despite this early religious intolerance these country people were kind, hospitable and very generous especially in times of distress, hardship and trials. Sorrows as well as happy occasions brought them together in warm fellowship. Nevertheless they mostly remained unquestioning on church doctrine and not seekers of further truth.

David was the third member of this family to espouse wholeheartedly the Bahá'í principles. Hilda and Rose wasted no time in informing their brother of these new ideas, writing and sending him pamphlets and books from Adelaide. David lived on a sheep-wheat farm called *Rockwood* ; in fact he and his younger brother, Frank, managed properties that included "*Parwingie*", a sheep-station on Eyre Peninsula, South Australia, "*Blue Hills*", a sheep property near Hammond, South Australia and some irrigation blocks for lucerne, near Orroroo, South Australia. Except for *Rockwood* these properties were sold later.

David Brooks and his mother, Margaret

The Great Depression of 1928-31 as well as droughts, seemingly frequent especially in the 1930's and 1940's, and the Second World War inflicted many hardships on these two brothers and their families as low prices for commodities and poor seasons resulted too often in mortgages and consequent worry and hardships. A mortgage meant being in debt to a bank or pastoral company and in those days, as I recall, that amounted to a disgrace, or so it seemed to my father; it certainly was a worry to him. These days taking out a mortgage is a widespread practice, regarded as a necessity for primary producers, home buyers and business people. During those mortgage years there was little spare cash and there was always the fear of being sold up by the pastoral company. However, that period of insecurity passed and my father entered reasonably prosperous years. Later David referred to those days of austerity and worry as a journey that prepared him to recognize and accept the Bahá'í Faith unreservedly.

Before his marriage to Amy Olive Mills, David was a lay preacher in the Methodist Church (now Uniting Church) and was probably visiting Amyton, a village some distance away, in that capacity when he met Amy playing the organ for the church service. He must have withdrawn from lay preaching in his early years of marriage or even before. He stopped going to church, remarking later that the clergy couldn't answer his many questions satisfactorily. So he delved into new ideas and theories, philosophies, science, `new thought', British Israelites and no doubt many other movements.

David Brooks and family.
L-R: Norman, David, Merle, Margaret, Amy.

David, I think, had always been an avid reader and while still young had attended King's College, Adelaide, for a brief period to further his education; there becoming absorbed in the English Classics, novels and poetry - Charles Dickens, Sir Walter Scott, Macaulay, Ruskin, Tennyson and others as well as acquiring appreciation of the great stature of Shakespeare. He wouldn't have claimed to have had a deep or wide knowledge of these writers but he loved the glimpses he had and passed that appreciation on to his three children whom he was keen to see educated. Accepting the Bahá'í Faith opened up new and wonderful horizons, a new stage in his life, giving him assurance, hope and purpose.

My brother, Norman Brooks, writes of our father thus:

"A man with an astute mind; well-read and could converse on many subjects. He fostered friendship with a great many people of various professions, from lawyers, bankers, industrialists (manufacturing industries), medical profession, botanists and also in his own field of agriculture and agronomy.

His attention to detail on his own property included his ability to breed the best stud Merinos possible, which involved his understanding of genetics and his ability to assess the qualities of the Merino for the best outcome in a breeding program. He was called upon to judge at many country shows.

The native flora of the area was of special interest to him; searching out the Botanical references and other details re their distribution over various climatic areas across Australia. The Allepo Pine, which was from the Mediterranean, he found to be a suitable shelter tree for his area, being one of the first to plant this tree around the homestead.

In his early years, he was a keen debater and took part in many of the local community activities. He was chairman of the Local Primary Producers Association, chairman of the local Institute and lay preacher in the Methodist Church.

When David became a Bahá'í, as will be described later, he announced this decision to the Church and friends - all Hell broke out! "He's gone over to Satan" his friends said. They pleaded, begged him - "No!" David replied, "There is more to life than just Methos."

David, Hilda, Rose and prize Merino sheep

As his family recall, it did not take him long to recognize and acknowledge the truth of the Bahá'í Faith and the claim of Bahá'u'lláh. He read the literature sent him by his sisters, keeping it handy on his desk for reference or study.

My sister Margaret, recalls her father telling her, when she was about ten years old, that he would be sorting and grading the shorn wool on the table in the shearing shed and thinking of these new, challenging principles and claims, and with the work done he would hurry back to the homestead to the books or pamphlets on his desk. At one stage of this investigation, she said, David caught the train from Booleroo Centre to Adelaide to visit Hilda and Rose and presumably, she understands, it was to discuss the Faith; and David wasn't one to go to the city for any but urgent reasons, such as business. I, myself, then about thirteen years old, remember my father having a short afternoon rest in the hall at *Rockwood*, and excitedly exclaiming "This is it. This is it!" He was reading *"The Unfoldment of World Civilization"* by Shoghi Effendi, then in booklet form as was *"The Goal of a New World Order"*.

He had accepted the Faith. We are not sure of the actual moment of acceptance but it was not a long drawn out investigation, perhaps a few months. He enthusiastically spoke to friends and acquaintances of this new Faith. He was well known and respected in the district and being a sheep-breeder had become successful in the yearly country and city shows where he was awarded championship prizes for his sheep on a number of occasions. To produce sheep with high quality wool was an ambition that brought him into contact with others and also he was a foundation trustee of the Booleroo Centre Institute and a member of the district Primary Industries Association. Thus, though an isolated believer, in a very conservative rural society he wasn't one to mind. He educated his three children who declared as Bahá'í youth and he freely spoke of Bahá'í principles to friends and acquaintances, enjoying such discussion and the sharing of jokes, for though serious by nature, he did love a good laugh and joke.

His close friends thought a lot of him though many others might have considered him a heretic, an enigma or even as an outcast of the 'fold'! He once told me that there was only one atheist in the district, indicating to me the extent of his teaching. To admit to being an atheist was rather unusual, for at that time such an open divergence from orthodox views was exceptional.

I owe my father so much. He loved the Bahá'í Writings and studied them deeply, introducing them to his children, his friends and many people in the district. My mother told me that I adored my father and while I was still a pre-school child would "track" him down when he and my mother were visiting local towns on market days or other occasions and being a shy child I would hide behind his long legs and peep out to see the sheep being marketed or whatever was going on!

At home I enjoyed visiting him at his work on the property, perhaps taking to him his morning tea or lunch. He enjoyed his work with the sheep and loved reading whether it be great literature, philosophical or scientific matter or new ideas.

After I married and was living in another State I saw him less often. Sometimes during vacations Jim, myself and our three children would visit *Rockwood* and we would delight in talking Bahá'í, sharing our understanding and experiences of this New Revelation to mankind.

Just a few years before he died, David retired to Adelaide in the suburb of Beaumont (4 Glenroy Avenue) to live with his wife, Amy, who accepted the Faith in her latter years. He was a member of Burnside Community but was then frail and suffering from Parkinson's disease. He died on the 9th of August, 1967 at the age of 83 leaving three active Bahá'í children, five active Bahá'í grandchildren, six active Bahá'í great-grandchildren and many other descendants not yet adult, but most being educated in these universal principles. His grave is in the Centennial Park Cemetery, Adelaide.

The Brooks Family property, Rockwood, in the 1930s

Amy Olive Brooks (née Mills)
28/3/1891 - 25/11/1977

My mother Amy Olive Mills was the daughter of a pioneering family who had gone north at the time of the opening up of new farming land near Amyton and Hammond in South Australia. Here she was born, the second daughter of Emily and William Mills, and here she grew up and was educated, taking part in the social and musical activities, such as choir, which largely circled around the church in those days. Numerous families of that district at that time were sincerely God-fearing people, of high ethical and moral standards whose word was their bond and such influences were always being recalled by Amy in later life.

As a young woman, she married David Books of Booleroo Centre, also the son of a pioneering family and here, at the family property of *Rockwood*, she brought up her three children and together with David, continued to take an active interest in local affairs. Amy was a foundation member and first president of The Mothers and Babies Association of that district; she was a foundation member of the Country Women's Association of the area and held office on a number of occasions.

During the 1930's David and Amy, among many of the Brooks' family, accepted the Bahá'í Faith, as did her children and grandchildren.

Amy had always been interested in community services; she loved helping people, giving them small gifts she had made herself, and carrying on an extensive correspondence with friends. She was artistic, she had studied pianoforte and singing as a girl, and had been offered a scholarship to study with a well-known Australian artist, one of the Ashtons, but due to lack of money at the time couldn't avail herself of it.

She was dearly loved by her family and grandchildren and it gave her great pleasure to see their dedication to the Bahá'í Faith. Her family and friends will always remember her loving kindnesses and her genuine concern and sympathy for other people's troubles, her helpfulness and generosity, her love for children and flowers. Their hearts are sad for their personal loss. May God bless her and cause her to "enter the garden of happiness" and "Behold" His "Splendours on the loftiest mount".

Amy died on the 25th of November, 1977. Her grave is in Centennial Cemetery, Adelaide, South Australia.

Frank Dempster Brooks
2/10/1886 - 14/9/1968

Frank and Gladys

Frank became a Bahá'í in the 1940's learning of it either from his brother or his sisters, accepting it with enthusiasm and imparting its principles whenever he could to his friends and acquaintances in the country districts where he and his family resided. Like other members of this family he attended the Methodist Church while young. I recall he ran a sheep station, called Parwingie, between Iron Knob and Whyalla on Eyre Peninsula and after that was sold he lived on the Blue Hills sheep property in the Flinders region; it was salt bush country. With my father I visited him, his wife, Gladys (née Cream) and their three children: Coral, Glen and Patson. My father, David, would periodically visit his brother Frank to discuss business relating to the management of the property and problems to do with the sheep. They were close friends. In fact the siblings of this generation were very affectionate and loyal.

Frank became a diabetic, grew frailer and worked under much stress. Blue Hills was sold and the family moved to Quorn (S.A.) where I visited him, when on a Bahá'í teaching trip in the late 1940's. He and Gladys, who also became a Bahá'í, held firesides and were always happy to teach the Faith. In the 1960's they retired to Adelaide and became members of the Campbelltown Bahá'í Community. Frank was born in 1886 and died 14th of September, 1968.

Family Group; L-R: Maud Brooks, Mary Nichols, Gladys Brooks, Frank Brooks, Coral Nichols, Ewart Thomas, Hilda Thomas, Rose Hawthorne, Jim Nichols, Mary-Anne Palliaer as a child

Mary-Anne Palliaer, Bahá'í grand-daughter of Frank and Gladys, writes some of her memories of happy times spent with them.

> "Sitting on the bar of my Grandfather's bike, with legs dangling, as if riding a horse side-saddle, he would dinky me up to the local hospital in Quorn, to feed the fowls: bran and pollen were on the menu.
> Then, it was into the maintenance area of the hospital to stoke up the boiler. These chores were all part of Grand-dad Brooks' life in the mid-north of South Australia after he left the land. The locals would be regularly called upon to use his skills in knife sharpening. Whenever I reflect back on the visits to Quorn in the 50's, loving memories flood back.
> Nanna Brooks always had something wonderful cooking on the wood stove and would always let me sample a little before it was served to the family, followed by a bear hug that would swallow me up.
> Granddad always had a grape-vine, laden with the sweetest grapes, which he would sample while still on the vine. He said he would be happy in heaven if there were grapes."

recollections   Sketches of Some Early Australian Bahá'ís

Marjorie Winifred Duncan (née Brooks)

18/12/1903 - 26/1/1996

Dawn, Marjorie's Bahá'í daughter, writes of her mother:

"Marjorie Duncan was born Marjorie Winifred Brooks on 18th of February, 1903, at the family home *Rockwood* not far from Booleroo Centre in South Australia. She was the youngest of nine surviving children, the first two being twins who died tragically in their first year. When Marjorie

39

was born, the oldest son, Albert, had already left home to marry and live in Western Australia.

When Marjorie was seven her father died, and later, when she was about fifteen, Marjorie with her mother, Margaret, and her sisters, Maud and Hilda, went to live in Dulwich in Adelaide. Marjorie went to high school in Adelaide in a building, which is now a centre for the arts in the city. After leaving school she lived "a life of leisure and fun", she said. The loves of her life at that time were horses (she used to ride to school on a horse when living at *Rockwood*) and tennis. Marjorie said she just lived for tennis and playing cards, and had no interest in anything else, not even marriage.

However, at the age of twenty-five she married Ken Duncan, an employee with the Commonwealth Bank. Their son, Colin, was born about three years later, and daughter, Dawn, about five years after that. By this time the family had moved to Melbourne in 1932 and then to Seymour, also in Victoria, in 1939.

When Marjorie first heard about the Faith from her sisters, Rose and Hilda, she did not take them seriously as they had been interested in a number of organizations and she just expected their interest to wane in time.

In 1939 Martha Root came to Melbourne and a meeting was arranged for her to speak. The Bahá'í members of the family came to Melbourne also and sat Marjorie down with them. After the address Martha spoke lovingly with Marjorie for a short time then was called away to meet someone else. Marjorie thought to herself: "That's all right. I'm not important", whereupon Martha returned and said forcefully, "You are important!" Marjorie was astounded that she had read her thoughts.

Her husband, Ken, was very angry when she told him she had been to a Bahá'í meeting. He was so against the Faith that she had to hide a prayer book she had been given and had to read the prayers and any other Bahá'í literature when he was away at work.

In 1942, the family moved to Sydney where Ken became a manager of a branch of the Commonwealth Bank in the suburb of Brighton-le-Sands. Marjorie went through much anguish because of Ken's opposition. In the midst of this time she had a dream. In the dream Bahá'u'lláh came to her and

Marjorie Duncan in the grounds of the Bahá'í House of Worship, Sydney.

said, "You must write letters! You must write letters!"

Marjorie was much comforted by the dream but it was not until her children had grown up, married and left Sydney to go home-front pioneering in Tamworth and Parkes, N.S.W. that she realized what Bahá'u'lláh's words meant. She was to write to her children letters with news and encouragement at the time when they were isolated from other Bahá'ís and it was her letters that helped to sustain them while they built up communities there.

However, being a lone Bahá'í in Brighton-le-Sands after joining the Faith was not easy for Marjorie. She had to go alone at night, catch a tram, then a train and then walk to the Bahá'í Centre in the city just to attend a Feast. Some years later when the Guardian asked the believers to form communities in their own council areas, there were four Bahá'ís in the Rockdale Council area and Marjorie, her daughter, Dawn, and son-in-law, Geoff, along with Mrs. Vada Frazer Paterson, became the founding members of Rockdale Bahá'í Community. Marjorie was to serve on the Rockdale Assembly for about three decades.

Ken Duncan died in 1957 and Marjorie lived alone for over thirty years.
As well as being an active believer in the Rockdale area, Marjorie was to serve as a guide at the Bahá'í House of Worship at Ingleside for many years. She also relieved the caretaker at the Temple grounds on at least one occasion.

Some of the highlights of her life were attending the Bahá'í World Congress in London in 1963, visiting the Guardian's grave, making a pilgrimage to Iran and Israel to visit the Holy Places, and attending conferences in Fiji and Hong Kong.

At the age of 86 Marjorie went to live in Carnarvon, Western Australia to live with Dawn and Geoff as a home-front pioneer. She passed away nearly seven years later, just three weeks before her 93rd birthday.

Marjorie was noted for her bright and smiling face, her love for the Bahá'í Writings and for the members of her family. She was very generous and caring, interested in what was happening in the world and in the local scene, right up to the end of her life."

(End of Dawn's portrayal of her mother)

Margaret Dempster Brooks
17/4/1856 - 22/11/1948

Margaret Dempster born on 17th of April, 1856 was the eldest child of Scottish parents who came out from Scotland and bought land at Tarcowie, S.A. where Margaret grew up. She married William Brooks 12/3/1878 in Jamestown (S.A.) and died 22nd of November, 1948 in Adelaide.

Margaret, the mother of her five Bahá'í children Rose, David (my father), Frank, Hilda and Marjorie, accepted the Faith on 9th of October, 1939 a few years after they did and quite unexpectedly.

Adelaide Bahá'í Community, in the late 1930's and in the 1940's, though still small in number, but growing, was active and included knowledgeable, capable members, several of whom were members of the National Spiritual

Assembly from its inception in 1934. One was Hilda Brooks, Margaret's daughter, National Secretary and member of the Adelaide community. It so happened that Hilda was giving regular public lectures on the Bahá'í principles - bi-monthly, as I remember, because Bertha Dobbins was also thus involved.

Hilda, in preparation, would make notes and even practise a talk on her mother as well as ask her where in the Bible were certain references, prophecies or quotes, etcetera that she could use, appropriately, in her talk.

Now, Margaret and her husband, William, had assiduously raised their family in the Christian Religion (Methodist version). Regular family readings of the Bible were a feature of the household, not to mention the requirement of attending Sunday church. Perhaps, even then, there were polite or unspoken queries, but no satisfactory answers, perhaps some were quietly bored but the readings went on and the family should have been well versed in the Bible lore.

Many years later, in Adelaide, Hilda would prepare her talks, lectures or addresses and had to seek help in matters relating to the Bible. Margaret was well able to help her.

What was Hilda's surprise when one day her mother said, "I want to be a Bahá'í!" I remember Hilda telling me this and she and Rose were absolutely delighted. Perhaps out of respect for their mother's age and her love of the Bible, they had never previously suggested she accept the Faith.

Margaret was an independent spirit. She was small, of medium height, with grey hair at that time and very distinguished-looking I thought. She was quiet, a loving grandma and very courteous. I have happy memories of gathering wild flowers with her on the hills at *Rockwood* when I was three years old and much later, before I married, of her demonstrating the making of gem-scones and pastry.

A veritable matriarch! But above all, a Bahá'í. Her grave is in Centennial Park Cemetery, Adelaide.

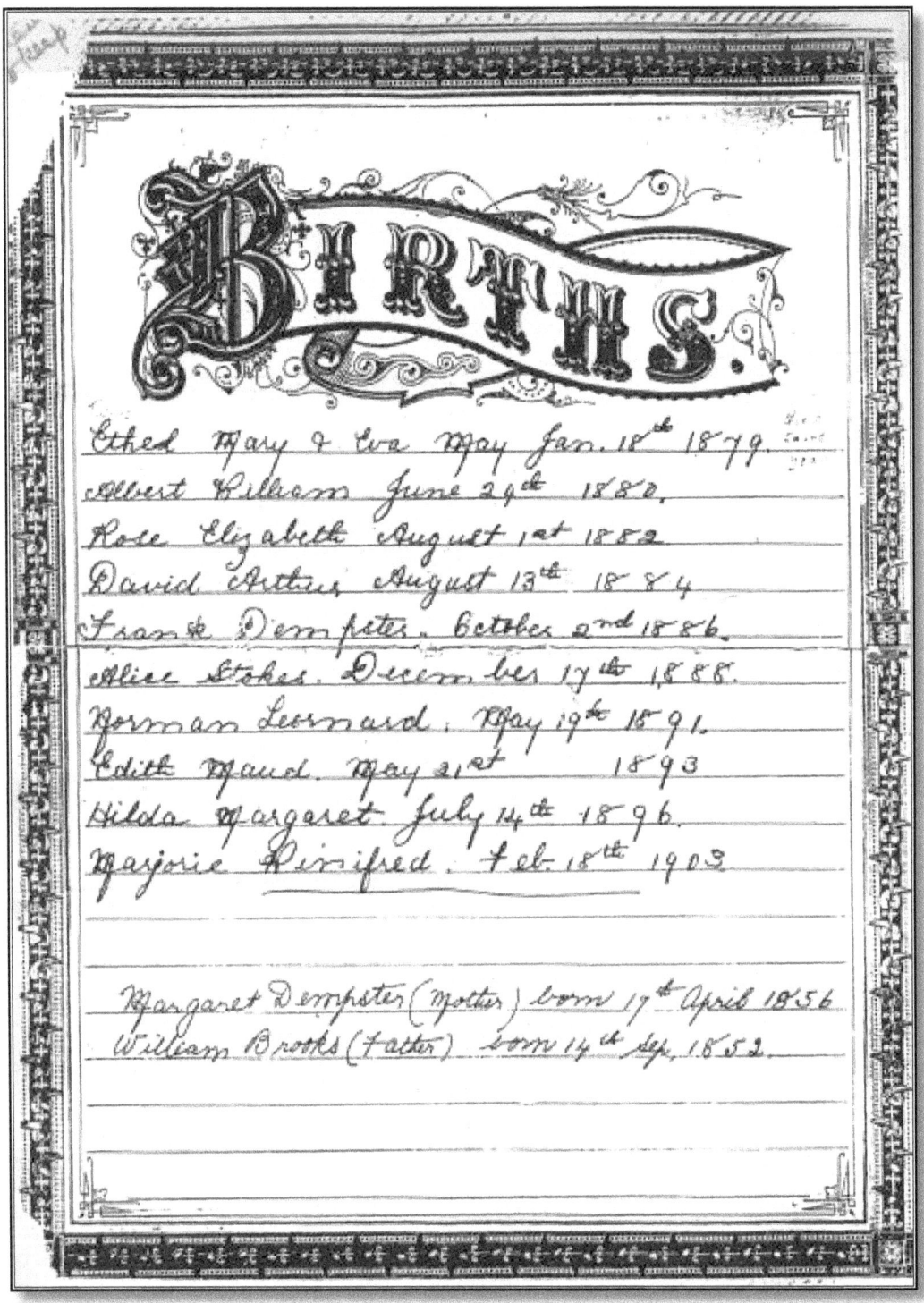

SECTION TWO

Second Generation Bahá'ís

James and Merle Heggie (née Brooks) in Sydney

Merle Olivia Heggie (née Brooks)
14/1/1920 -

Membership

I think I considered myself a Bahá'í in my early teens, being an isolated believer in the district of Booleroo Centre, South Australia. However, my father told me I couldn't attend Feasts in Adelaide if I did not sign a declaration card, so I signed in January 1937 at the age of 17 and went to the city to continue my education.

Reasons leading to the acceptance of the Faith

I remember the Faith appealed to me through its principle of "Progressive Revelation". It was "modern" - for today and tomorrow. What I heard in church and Sunday school seemed old-fashioned, centuries old, without joy or an interesting future! To accept Bahá'u'lláh's claim as the Manifestation for today was a natural step in my life.

Teachers

First my father, then my Aunt Hilda Brooks and Aunt Rose Hawthorne (née Brooks) taught me the Faith. I lived at the home of Rose and Uncle Will Hawthorne when I first lived in Adelaide. Rose held youth firesides, monthly, in her home, encouraging me to take friends and acquaintances to these firesides whom I met mostly at Adelaide University, encouraging me to study the Teachings, to hold the Fast, etcetera.

In those days Uncle Will would take us (Hilda, Rose, Grandma and me) for drives in his rather stately De Soto motor car around picturesque areas, such as the lovely fields and avenues of almond blossom in Spring. These fields are now housing estates. There was much conversation about the Faith especially when there were messages from the Guardian that Hilda received as National Secretary. Later, after my marriage in August 1947 to James Heggie, I have to add Jim as one of my teachers; certainly my deepening progressed through him.

Wedding of Merle and James Heggie August 1947
L-R : Lilly Brown (James Heggie's aunt who became a Bahá'í in early 1970's)
James Heggie, Merle Heggie, Hilda Thomas and Ewart Thomas

Travel Teaching

In 1949 I went on a few days visit to Quorn and Port Augusta, S.A. Activities there included a fireside at Frank and Gladys Brooks' home, meeting the sister of Irene Williams at Irene's request and presenting Bahá'í literature to various people.

Also, in 1949 I spent nine weeks in Toowoomba, Qld following up contacts that had previously been introduced to the Faith. At that time I accepted the job of casual teacher of piano pupils in Glennie Girls' Memorial School. While working in Kapunda, S.A. in 1943, I organized two public lectures with Bahá'í speakers: Hilda Brooks and Harold Fitzner coming from Adelaide; these were attended by local citizens; one meeting included three of the clergy from different churches. Irene Jackson (later Williams) there heard of the Faith and became a Bahá'í and pioneered to Fiji.

In 1975 after attending the U.K. Convention as a visitor I spent some weeks travel teaching in the south of England with my son Adrian - arranged by the National Teaching Committee of the U.K. contacting isolated believers as suggested by the N.T.C. of U.K.

Academia

- B.A. (Adelaide University);
- A.M.U.A. (music) (Adelaide Conservatorium);
- Secondary School Teacher - Certificate (Adelaide Teachers' College).

Communities I've lived and worked in

1. Adelaide
2. Kapunda (as an Isolated believer)
3. Sydney
4. Brisbane
5. Hurstville
6. Hunter's Hill
7. Blue Mountains
8. Ryde

After my marriage I belonged to the Sydney Bahá'í Community for one year, September 1947 to 1948, while Jim was secretary of the National Spiritual Assembly of Australia and New Zealand and we lived at the then National Headquarters, 2 Lang Road, Paddington, where I was hostess for that time.

Home Front Pioneering

In August 1948 Jim and I moved to Queensland to help Brisbane to achieve Assembly status. There were three members: Mr. Jack Bedgood, his mother Mrs. Bedgood and a Mr. Stewart who I think had first heard of the Faith on reading about 'Abdu'l-Bahá's visit to London in a Brisbane newspaper. This was a part of the Guardian's six-year plan for Australia. Brisbane L.S.A. was formed in 1949.

Serving on Local Spiritual Assemblies

- Brisbane, Qld from 1949 to early 1954;
- Hunter's Hill, NSW when it was formed in September 1976 with the help of two of our children, Jennifer and Adrian and their Bahá'í spouses (David Pepperell and Melanie Price). Worked in this community until August 1997 when I moved out selling my home, as Jim had passed on in August 31, 1992. Temporarily (6 months) I lived in Blue Mountains, later in April 1998 I bought a villa at 2/17 Kemp Street, Tennyson, NSW where I am now in the Ryde Community.

Committees

- Adelaide Youth Committee - I helped reform this with Lucy Truman (Giordano) and Margaret Brooks (later Chittleborough) and other members; I was a member from 1937 to 1942, I think. There had been active youth in Adelaide in the early 1930's (See *"The Bahá'í World"* 1932-1934, Vol. V, Page 379).

The Adelaide Youth Group was formed in 1937 under the guidance of Hilda Brooks, the N.S.A. Secretary and member of the Adelaide Spiritual Assembly.

Of this group, only two continued in the Faith. Those being: Lucy Giordano (née Lucy Truman) and Merle Heggie (née Merle Brooks). A few years saw the enrolment in our youth group of my sister Margaret Chittleborough (née Margaret Brooks), Avilda Reid (then née Johansson) and Jim Chittleborough. My brother Norman Brooks became a Bahá'í youth in 1941 but was always in an isolated area of South Australia.

Gradually the youth group grew with new members and Bahá'í children declaring. This growth became obvious after World War II.

- National Youth Committee

- Bahá'í House of Worship Service Committee from the first service after the Dedication in September 1961 for many years with some breaks. I was not on this committee while conductor of the Temple Choir.

- Bahá'í Temple Choir - I organized and conducted the Bahá'í Temple Choir for nearly nine years. In May 1966 the N.S.A. had accepted a Convention recommendation that a Temple choir be formed, so efforts were made towards this end viz. find suitable music and assemble singers. This resulted in the first two performances on the 6th of September, 1966 and the 13th of September, 1966; some music composed especially for the choir by Dorothy Stoney. Mary-Ann McLeod (Mary-Ann Chance Peters) provided a three-part harmony to "Yá Bahá'u'l-Abhá", the melody being composed by Saffa Kinney.

- For one service at the Temple in Langenheim, Germany, I conducted a choir after a quick get-together and a short practice. There was no permanent choir in Langenheim at that time. I had been invited to stay for ten days for this purpose by the Secretary of the N.S.A of Germany, whom I met when visiting that Temple on my way home from England in 1975.

- Served on many "short-lived" committees dealing with short-term projects.

- I was editor for "Herald of the South" for a short time, until production was stopped so all energies and time could go into achieving the Ten-Year Crusade. I was editor, as far as I can ascertain, from October 1957 to July 1960.

- Served as assistant for propagation to the Auxiliary Board member, David Hassall in the early 1980's.

First Bahá'í Temple choir
Top L-R : Merle Heggie (conductor), Sue Sale, Kathy Sale,
Wanita Buckney, Erica Salter. Seated : Julia Salter, Jennifer Heggie

Guiding at the Bahá'í House of Worship

I have been involved with this activity on a regular and frequent basis from the time of its Dedication in 1961. At present, I guide one day a month as well as with my Community when rostered to guide or do "maintenance" and as a supervisor at intervals to help new guides.

Books that guided and educated me in my early years (not including the Sacred Writings)

- "Bahá'u'lláh and the New Era" by Dr. J.E. Esslemont;
- "Security for a Failing World" by Stanwood Cobb;
- "The Bahá'í Proofs" by Mirzá Abúl-Fazl.

Meeting Hands of the Cause of God

(Listed in chronological order as appointed by the Guardian)

1. Martha Root - who invited me and my father to her room in the Grosvenor Hotel, Adelaide, where she talked to us and gave us books: a prayer book, the latest Bahá'í World Volume and a silk scarf.
2. Alí-Akbar Furútan - when he visited Brisbane.
3. Ugo Giachery
4. Dhikru'll'áh Khádem
5. Clara Hyde Dunn
6. Amatu'l-Bahá Rúhíyyih Khánum, who visited us at our home, 20 Milling Street, Gladesville during Temple Dedication in 1961.
7. Agnes Alexander
8. Enoch Olinga
9. William Sears
10. John Robarts
11. Collis Featherstone
12. Rahmatu'lláh Muhájir
13. Abu'l-Qásim Faizí who had visited us in Brisbane with Hand of the Cause Mr. Furutan, but Mr. Faizi was not a Hand of the Cause at the time.

Some Highlights

- Attending the Bahá'í World Congress in London, 1963;
- Visiting Shoghi Effendi's grave;
- Visiting the Bahá'í House of Worship, Wilmette, 1963;
- The bounty of pilgrimage in April 1975;
- Visiting the House of Bahá'u'lláh in Tehran, 1975;
- Visiting the House of the Báb in Shiraz, 1975 and going to the mosque where the Bab spoke from the pulpit;

- Visiting city of Isfahan in Iran, meeting Bahá'ís, attending a youth meeting there and staying a night in the Eastern Pilgrimage House;

In April 1958 the Sydney Intercontinental Conference was held and the Guardian's representative brought to Sydney holy relics to be laid in the very foundation of our Temple. Those relics were: a bag of dust from the Shrine of Bahá'u'lláh and some plaster from the Bab's fortress at Mahku; both these precious relics were enclosed in silver caskets and at a simple ceremony during the Conference were laid in the foundation by Hand of the Cause, Clara Dunn. Jim Heggie, a member of the N.S.A. at the time, placed one of those precious relics in my silver jewel box, and with the other, they were suitably laid in the Mashriqu'l-Adhkar with many spiritual significances relating to this World Faith.

Plaque in honour of the Sacred relics laid in the foundation of the Bahá'í House of Worship in Sydney

It has been a great pleasure to see the establishment and growth of the education of children in the school scripture classes in which, not only Bahá'í children are involved but non-Bahá'í children, at the wishes of their parents. In earlier days when Dr. Ray Meyer was working on a religious curriculum and working towards its acceptance in schools, I had the pleasure, with Fahimeh Walker, of making a presentation to a Supervisor of education in N.S.W. (whose name and exact position I cannot now recall) the Bahá'í literature relating to children's education. It was but a small step we feel in the ultimate acceptance of the Bahá'í teachers being involved in children's religious classes in the school curriculum. Fahimeh and I were happy with the interview and the privilege of this early task.

Conferences attended

1. Attending in 1944, the Centenary of the Báb's Declaration held in Adelaide; and participating in the programme;
2. Sydney - International Conference, 1967;
3. Canberra - International Conference, 1982;
4. Sydney - Centenary of the Passing of Bahá'u'lláh held in Darling Harbour Convention Centre, 1992.

Early Believers I remember

Some of those early staunch Bahá'ís I recall and whom I met later were Mrs. Silver Jackman (chairman of the first N.S.A.) and Mr. Robert Brown (treasurer of the first N.S.A.), Mr. Joe Dobbins and Mrs. Bertha Dobbins, Mr. Harold Fitzner and Mrs. Florence Fitzner, Miss Ethel Dawe (all of Adelaide) and in Sydney: Mr. Oswald Whitaker (the first Australian Bahá'í and known to his friends as "Whit").

A very close friend of Jim and mine, Mrs. Jane Routh raised in a very Catholic family that included a priest, became a Bahá'í in the early 1930's. Her family considered her a lost soul, so they prayed for her hoping she would return to the Catholic Faith.

Mr. Stanley W. Bolton and Mrs. Mariette Bolton and joining, I think a few years later, Mrs. Jean Hutchinson-Smith, Miss Gladys Moody, Miss Linda Banfield, Mr. Noel Walker and Mrs. Bessie Walker.

There was Miss Effie Baker, recognized as the first woman Bahá'í in Australia, who joined the Faith at the same time as Miss Ruby Beaver (known as "Peter"). Effie spent many years serving in the Holy Land and returned to Australia in 1937. As the years passed, there were many others who joined and served the Faith.

I pay loving tribute to both my parents: my mother, Amy Brooks (née Mills) who became a Bahá'í in her latter years and my father, David Arthur Brooks, a deepened, well-read and devoted Bahá'í. Both encouraged me in my education and were loving, supportive parents. I owe much to them.

Merle and James Heggie

Margaret Maud Chittleborough (née Brooks)

Born: 2/6/1923

Margaret, the second daughter of David and Amy Brooks, grew up at *Rockwood* attending Primary and High Schools in Booleroo Centre and being taught the Bahá'í Faith by her father. She happily declared at fifteen and was the first isolated Bahá'í youth of that district. After graduating at High School she went to Adelaide in 1940 and became an active and early member of the Adelaide Youth Group.

She recalls having wonderful support and encouragement from both Aunts (Rose Hawthorne and Hilda Brooks) and the older members of Adelaide at the Bahá'í meetings in Epworth Building (city) and home firesides.

Margaret worked as a dental nurse until she married John James Chittleborough, February 1946. During the 1950's they moved to the south east of South Australia and lived in Narracourt and later in Mount Gambier. They had two sons, David born 8/04/1947 and Andrew born 6/07/1951, both brought up as Bahá'ís. Jim worked as a physiotherapist. Margaret and Jim were able to speak to residents about the Faith and hold meetings when possible.

Jim Chittleborough

About 1965 they returned to Adelaide, settling in Enfield where an Assembly was formed, Margaret and Jim serving on that LSA for a number of years. David and Andrew, their two children, graduated in the local High School, going on to the University of Adelaide.

As the house and garden in Enfield became too large for them to maintain satisfactorily and Bahá'í activities ever-increasing, they moved to a unit in

Tranmere and became active members of the Campbelltown Community, S.A. serving on the Local Assembly for some years.

Margaret and Jim Chittleborough and baby David in 1947

Margaret and Jim Chittleborough in later years

It is appropriate here to mention Jim's other Bahá'í activities. He served in the Army Medical Corps, as a soldier during World War II in New Guinea and Borneo. His brother-in-law, James Heggie, also served in the Army in New Guinea during World War II. After being discharged in 1945 he qualified as a physiotherapist at Adelaide University, practising in his clinic in North Adelaide, and at his Enfield house. He also helped in Domiciliary Work at Northfield Hospital. What is specially important is his Bahá'í service on the Continental Pioneer Committee and as Marriage Celebrant, dedicating many years to both of these Bahá'í needs and supported by Margaret in these demanding services to the Faith.

Margaret and Jim had the joy of pilgrimage in 1977, first going to Iran, visiting the House of Bahá'u'lláh in Tehran, then going to Isfahan and Shiraz and then on to the Holy Land, a memorable blessing.

Margaret always supported whole-heartedly any project, task or responsibility, whether personal, social or Bahá'í, that came her way and was necessary to undertake. She enjoyed making a happy, comfortable and well organized home and tending the early lives of her children with full care and attention to their development and education, Bahá'í and academic.

The Principle of equality for men and women has been and still is gradually being accepted, as well as a growing perception and realization in society of its implications. Margaret, being educated from childhood as a Bahá'í was well aware and appreciative of this principle. Without a family, Margaret might well have carried out a successful career in the business world. However, in those years, 1940's and 1950's, Margaret gave her full attention and time to making the home happy and orderly. When the children started school she was free to work part time to help with Jim's patients. The urge for a career to the detriment (usually) of the children was not an issue for Margaret. Of course, those times were less pressing to women in this respect. This principle can surely be observed with or without a career. Nevertheless women, today, are having to prove that they are as capable as men in the workplace. As time goes on the situation for women with careers will surely not be to the detriment of children.

Margaret is a caring person and has been successful and happy in any work she has done.

NORMAN DAVID BROOKS
2/1/1926 -

Norman and his family; L-R: Simone, Norman, baby Rebecca, David, Helen and Julianne, 1972.

Norman became a Bahá'í signing a declaration card in 1941, his father David, having taught him from an early age, along with his two sisters, about the Revelation of Bahá'u'lláh.

He was the youngest of the three children of David and Amy, being an isolated youth at the time of his declaration.

Norman graduated at Booleroo Centre High School and continued to live on the sheep/wheat property where he grew up, not being free to further his scholastic education in Adelaide, as the great Depression of 1928-31 and World War II were inhibiting factors to leaving the land. Being an only son on the land he wasn't enlisted in the Australian Army. It is hardly necessary to say that he has loved his life on the property working hard, improving the land by planting more trees (began by his father), developing suitable pastures and beautifying the homestead surroundings.

After his father David passed on, the responsibility was his. To improve *Rockwood's* financial viability more land was acquired *viz. Mookra* a property in the foothills of the Flinders Range and some at Yandiah a few miles from *Rockwood*.

Like his father before him, Norman an isolated believer, has taught the Bahá'í Faith fearlessly and continuously in this country district. Norman has led a social and well-integrated life in the district at *Rockwood*, home of his ancestors. He always speaks about the Faith to anyone interested; has held occasional formal firesides, attended, at times, meetings and Feasts in other communities in Crystal Brook, Port Pirie, Melrose, and in communities in Adelaide and Sydney. Visits to the latter city have given him the opportunity to attend services in the Bahá'í House of Worship. He enjoyed the International Conference in Canberra in 1982.

Norman taught the Faith to his four children, who were also taken by their mother, a strong Methodist Church member, to church and Sunday school. Although none of them have yet accepted the Faith, Norman's teaching and influence will surely one day bear fruit.

He has encountered strong opposition at times amongst the many conservative people of his district but being dedicated and steadfast in his faith and with a strong character, that has not deterred him. Many know of the Faith through Norman or his father. It is interesting that he has had at least three Christian clergy learning of the Faith from him and asking for more information. One of them even said he would be a Bahá'í if he were not already a clergyman! Another clergyman became a close and valued friend.

Norman has participated in many district activities. He was chairman of the committee that arranged a big function to commemorate the centenary of the founding of Booleroo Centre in 1975. It was quite an important state event, well organized and supported. The occasion was attended by the then Governor of South Australia, Sir Marcus Oliphant, well-known scientist and other personages of note.

He has, through the years, worked on the following organizations at various times:

- Institute - now called "Civic Centre"
- Booleroo Centre Primary School
- Booleroo Centre High School
- Scouts
- Primary Producers Association
- Booleroo Centre Primary School Centenary
- Booleroo Centre Town Centenary
- Melrose Pony Club
- Booleroo Centre Youth Club (now disbanded)

It is hard to assess the effect of Bahá'u'lláh's Revelation on this conservative district but it is obvious that many of its precepts have had their effect, leading people to a broader understanding of humanity, of social issues and requirements and even in some, a more tolerant view of religion.

Rockwood in the 1990's

recollections   Sketches of Some Early Australian Bahá'ís

COLIN WILLIAM DUNCAN

5 /11/1930 - 8 /8/1987

Colin Duncan with his mother Marjorie

The following article is supplied by Allaine Duncan-Fish and her daughter Ruth Park.

"Colin Duncan had been raised Presbyterian, attended a church youth group and was heavily involved in the Boy Scout Movement. Through contact via his mother Marjorie Duncan (née Brooks) and sister Dawn, Colin became acquainted with the Faith.

In the year 1955, Colin Duncan declared himself a Bahá'í and shortly after, married Allaine Whitehouse. Their Bahá'í marriage took place at 2 Lang

Road, Paddington, the first National Bahá'í headquarters at which Mother Dunn attended and read a lovely prayer. Around 1956 Colin and Allaine moved to Tamworth, N.S.W.

Colin moved from Sydney to Tamworth following directives of the Guardian for Bahá'ís to pioneer into the country. He pioneered to Tamworth until 1969 having many wonderful visitors such as Hand of the Cause of God, Collis Featherstone as well Enoch Olinga, Frank Khan, Thelma Perks and many visitors from overseas such as Israeli Rathyle. As a radio host for the ABC Radio Women's Program in Tamworth, Allaine would interview as many as she could.

Allaine had initially been antagonistic towards the Faith coming from a staunch Salvation Army background. Her eldest brother was an officer in the Army and her father conducted the band in the main Army Hall in Sydney. He also composed a number of very well known musical works for the Army. As a result of this antagonism Colin was forced to say his prayers in the bathroom. Allaine, intending to prove the falsity of the Bahá'í Faith began reading Bahá'í writings, and it was then that she also became a Bahá'í after meeting Stanley P. Bolton while visiting his chiropractic clinic.

During their time in Tamworth three of their four children were born. (Stephen 1957, Ruth 1960, Fiona 1963) Rose garden classes were regularly conducted where the children attended. A number of locals became Bahá'ís. At this time the Bahá'í community in Australia was very small and everyone knew everyone else. Visits to the Temple were times to reconnect with old friends. Colin during this time in Tamworth worked for the Commonwealth Bank. At night he went to TAFE studying accountancy. In 1969 the family moved to Sydney for one year where the family lived with Marjorie Duncan (Colin's mother) in Brighton Le Sands and then he proceeded to Dubbo.

About the time they moved to Dubbo, NSW they had three children: Stephen, Ruth and Fiona then their 4th child, Glen was born in 1971. They remained as pioneers in Dubbo and formed an Incorporated Assembly in 1975.

At that time Dubbo was a small rural town five hours drive west of Sydney with a population of 15,000 people. Here Colin worked as an accountant and set about proclaiming the advent of Bahá'u'lláh. Ads were placed in the local newspaper inviting people to hear about his new message. A number of people came to his home to hear. Eventually enough declared to establish a Local Spiritual Assembly in 1975, which was later incorporated. Now in the year 2007 this Assembly remains incorporated.

Colin and Allaine Duncan

Colin would visit many isolated locations such as Wilcannia, Bourke, Coonabarabran, Gilgandra, Wellington, etc. where he would arrange public notice of public meetings in local halls.

For many years he did the accountancy books for the N.S.A. of Australia until just before his death at the age of 57 in 1987, August 8. He was known and respected within the community as a wonderful man and his infectious laughter was renowned. Modest and dedicated, his home was always open. He was endowed with a special quality that attracted and endeared him to people.

One Christmas holidays a large number of Vietnamese "boat people" refugees were taken from the immigrant hostels in Sydney to stay as guests at Colin and Allaine's home in Dubbo. Colin arranged paid employment at Auscott where they were able to work on the cotton, and save to start a new life. Contact was maintained and Colin was later invited to many of the new immigrants' weddings and special occasions, etc.

Aboriginal girls from towns further west would stay as Colin and Allaine's guests whilst studying at TAFE in Dubbo for short periods. At a time when Dubbo was predominantly white Anglo-Saxon, the Duncan's home was a place where a constant stream of visitors and guests from all around the world would be passing. This was one feature that distinguished their home from all the rest.

Colin passed away in 1987 and was buried in the Bahá'í section of the Dubbo Cemetery. This has now been changed to be a non-denominational cemetery."

Dawn Rose Dibdin (née Duncan)

16/8/1935 -

The following article is supplied by Dawn Rose Dibdin (née Duncan).

"My mother, Marjorie Duncan (née Brooks), became a Bahá'í when I was about eleven, but she could not talk much about the Teachings as my father was annoyed that a member of his family was involved in something unusual. I was happily involved with the Presbyterian Sunday School and youth fellowship but some remarks my mother made caused me to question some of the Christian interpretation of prophecy.

At eighteen I attended a talk given by Mr. Furutan, and translated by Mr. Faizi, at the Bahá'í Headquarters, 2 Lang Road, Paddington. That night and on subsequent days Mr. Faizi and I discussed the Teachings and they made so much sense. Five months later, in May, 1954, I became a Bahá'í.

In the meantime Geoff, my future husband, was studying the Teachings in New Guinea where he was working for Qantas. He also joined in May, 1954. Two years later we married in May 1956.

We were soon appointed on to the National Youth Committee, and Geoff on to the National Publicity Committee, feeling a bit out of our depth. When Shoghi Effendi asked the believers to form communities in the council areas in which they lived, my mother, Geoff and I, along with another believer, formed the first Bahá'í community of Rockdale. Later Geoff and I moved to Gymea Bay and for a short time became members of Caringbah Spiritual Assembly.

In 1959 we moved to Parkes, NSW, with two little children (Colin and Marjorie), where Geoff continued to work as an accountant. Parkes had only one Chinese and one Aboriginal family and no other nationalities. Nearly everyone was at least nominally Christian, and we soon realized there was a big job ahead, and we ourselves needed to learn a lot more about the Faith.

In the early days there Geoff joined the Old People's Welfare Association and I joined Meals on Wheels. As time went by we became part of the music scene in Parkes, playing in concerts and for musicals put on by the Musical and Dramatic Society and were even asked by the Catholic church to play for some of their music nights. I played piano and Geoff violin.

By this time our youngest, Linda was born and I began taking on music students for the piano, studying music myself at the Convent at the same time. Then, around 1964 we had the opportunity to run a short Bahá'í programme on radio every week, which we continued all the years we were there. Preparing for these programmes meant that we spent hours each week studying the Bahá'í teachings until we had a fairly good understanding of many aspects of the Faith. Another major project was to put on Bahá'í displays at the Parkes Annual Shows.

In 1963 I started weekly classes at the Retarded Children's School where I had been invited to give the children some basic religious instruction and musical activities. This went on for eight years until we moved in 1971. Geoff became involved with the newly formed branch of the United Nations Association in 1967 as secretary.

My other involvements in the town were with the Horticultural Society, school parents' organization and a women's discussion group.

It took until 1968 before we had new believers. This followed a memorable night (27 November, 1967) when we held a public meeting with Niu Tuataga from Samoa giving a talk, and a CBS film "And His Name Shall Be One" from the Lamp Unto My Feet series, which had been shown on North American television. The write-up of this meeting is in a copy of the local newspaper, which was placed in a time capsule, and will be opened fifty years from that week!

The first Spiritual Assembly of the Bahá'ís of Parkes was formed at Ridván 1970 by seven local people and ourselves. More people became believers. Then, Geoff lost his job and we moved to Griffith in Southern NSW in 1971.

In Griffith we lived in an old farmhouse for a few years. We were quite close to an Aboriginal housing reserve and became friends with the local Aboriginal people resulting in our joining the Griffith Aboriginal Advancement Organization and becoming chairperson and secretary.

While still at the farmhouse we held the first Griffith Youth Camp (Easter 1974), which was intended to bring together all the Bahá'í youth of the Riverina but actually attracted youth from as far away as Sydney, Dubbo, Canberra and Adelaide. These continued for a further twelve years well after we had moved away.

At this time we placed (as we understand) the first Bahá'í advertisement on television in Australia! This was in addition to Bahá'í ads in the local paper.

Geoff and I both spent some years on the Riverina Regional Teaching Committee and hosted several regional conferences in our home.

Dawn and Geoff with children Colin and Marjorie in Parkes, NSW, 1960

Dawn and husband Geoff in Carnarvon, WA, 1991

The first Spiritual Assembly of Griffith was formed after about five years (1976), with a mixture of homefront pioneers and local believers.

Our contact with Aboriginal people continued with Aboriginal children attending children's classes in large numbers, and some adults attending the many firesides and get-togethers.

In 1979 Marjorie, our daughter, and I went on the first of two two-week travel-teaching trips to Lord Howe Island. The second trip took place about two years later.

After we had lived ten years in Griffith, my mother asked if we would look after her sisters, Rose and Maud, who were living in Adelaide, both in nursing homes but needing assistance.

In December 1980 Linda and I moved to Adelaide, Geoff joining us in March, 1981. Colin and Marjorie had already left home to go to university.

Geoff and I were elected on the Burnside Assembly of which Aunt Hilda had been a foundation member years before in the fifties. Geoff found work with the Guide Dogs for the Blind Association and I resumed music teaching.

In April 1982 Geoff, Linda and I went on Pilgrimage to the Bahá'í World Centre, Geoff returning in 1992 for the Centenary of the Passing of Bahá'u'lláh.

For over eight years my life was taken up with visiting Aunt Rose and Aunt Maud, giving music lessons and working as secretary to the Burnside Bahá'í Community. As well as being chairperson of Burnside, Geoff served as secretary of the RTC and as an Assistant to the Auxiliary Board for Protection.

After Maud and Rose died and Linda left to marry, my mother, Marjorie, came to live with us. In that year I too was appointed an Assistant for Protection.

Our time in Adelaide came to an end when we (Marjorie Duncan, Geoff and I) moved to Carnarvon, in the north of Western Australia in May 1989 to assist with Aboriginal teaching. Marjorie, our daughter, and her husband, Peter Tidman, had already been, serving the Faith there for six years.

In Carnarvon Geoff found the ideal job for getting in contact with the many Aboriginal people of the area as accountant for KARU, an organization which looked after the financial affairs of a number of Aboriginal groups. His fellow workers and his boss were all Aboriginal people.

Once again my life was bound up with Assembly secretarial work, music students and looking after my mother who was quite elderly and frail by this time (in her late eighties). I was also Assistant for Protection for all of the North West and an advisor for the National Bahá'í Education Committee. For a time I assisted with a literacy programme at Carnarvon High School, and for many years was a volunteer for the Family Support Service. In April 1995, Geoff retired and in January 1996 my mother died. We moved further north to Karratha in 1997 and shared a home with Marjorie and Peter Tidman and two of our grandchildren, Natasha and Raymond, for two years.

Karratha was unbearably hot for almost twelve months of the year. The way to meet people was to have children at school, or join a sporting or church group, none of which seemed possible for us, otherwise people stayed indoors and tried to keep cool. Geoff worked for six months as a consultant for an Aboriginal Health service in Roebourne, but other than that we found it difficult to make contacts. Geoff's health deteriorated and we realized we would have to live closer to better medical attention, so in April 1999 we moved back to South Australia to Mount Barker not far from Adelaide.

We are both currently serving on the Mount Barker LSA."

Pen sketch supplied by Dawn Rose Dibdin (née Duncan).

Dawn and her mother Marjorie arrive at Carnarvon, WA, as Bahá'í pioneers in 1989

Geoff and Dawn with Aboriginal elder Slim Parker and his wife Susan Hughes, Onslow, WA

Dawn with Bahá'í children's class Griffith, NSW

Dawn outside family home in Rose Park, Adelaide. Hilda Brooks and her mother Margaret lived here for many years. Hilda was NSA secretary when she lived here.

recollections Sketches of Some Early Australian Bahá'ís

Jim and Merle Heggie participating in the SIX-YEAR PLAN 1948-1953

It was rather overwhelming to be part of the Six-year Plan. Jim and I happily set off from Sydney in August, 1948 for Brisbane by train, second class. We had very little money. Jim had been demobilized in 1947 after 5 years in the Australian Army. He was familiar with the city of Brisbane, not Hobart, also a goal, which I might have preferred. However, having spent several years in New Guinea while a soldier during World War II, Jim was acclimatized to a warm climate. Another inducement to go to Brisbane was the successful and recent visit as travel teachers to that city of my two Aunts, Hilda Thomas and Rose Hawthorne.

But in recalling our efforts in this new major teaching plan it is appropriate first to refer to Shoghi Effendi's guidance at the time. His communications were always special, beyond evaluation, giving us guidance, encouragement and inspiration to serve. Thus I have selected quotations from his letters and cables to the N.S.A of Australia and New Zealand that refer to this Six-year Plan that was formed, pursued and achieved by the friends in response to our beloved Guardian's wishes. They are as follows, in chronological sequence.

In a letter on behalf of the Guardian, dated 14th of March, 1947, Rúhíyyih Khánum wrote:

"He feels very strongly that the main thing for your Assembly and all the believers of both Australia and New Zealand to concentrate on are teaching plans. The United States, India, Persia and England are all embarked on ambitious and bold teaching campaigns, and it is a great pity that Australia, where the Cause is now firmly established and boasts an active National Assembly, should not have a definite plan, with fixed goals, of its own.

When the believers are embarked on a definite teaching schedule there will be less time for them to constantly occupy themselves with purely secondary administrative points of procedure. Teaching is their need, the solution to any problems they may feel they have.

He was delighted over the report of the work in Brisbane; this is a step in the right direction, and should be followed through vigorously. Please convey to those who have devotedly served there and brought this group into being his warm thanks and his admiration for their services.

You may be sure he deeply values the loyal and persevering efforts of your Assembly to promote the Faith in all its aspects in Australia and New Zealand. His loving prayers are offered on your behalf and for the success of your labours.

With loving Bahá'í greetings,
R. Rabbani"

And in Shoghi Effendi's words in that letter:

"Dear and valued co-workers:

I wish to appeal, through you, to the members of the entire community in both Australia and New Zealand, to arise, in these opening years of the Second Bahá'í century, and, lend, through their concerted, their sustained, and determined efforts, an unprecedented impetus to the growth of the Faith, the multiplication of its administrative centres, and the consolidation of its nascent institutions. The initiation of a Plan, carefully devised, universally supported, and designed to promote effectively the vital interests of the Faith, and attain a definite objective within a specified number of years, would seem, at the present hour, highly desirable and opportune, and will, as a magnet, attract, to an unprecedented degree, the blessings of Bahá'u'lláh on the members of both communities, both individually and collectively.

Now that the structural basis of the Bahá'í Administrative Order has been firmly and definitely laid in these far-away lands, and the National Headquarters of that Order established, a systematic effort must be exerted to widen the basis of that Order, by multiplying the Administrative institutions and forming the necessary nuclei, which, as they develop and are consolidated, will have to be utilized as the divinely ordained and most effectual instruments for the proclamation of the Faith to the masses.

I fully realize how small are your numbers, how circumscribed are your means, how vast the distances that separate the centres already established. But I firmly believe that the initiation of a Plan to remedy the very deficiencies from which the infant Administrative Order is now suffering, and a firm resolve to carry out its provisions, as well as a sustained effort to make the necessary sacrifices for its consummation, will set in motion forces of such magnitude, and draw upon both communities blessings of such potency, as shall excite the wonder of the believers themselves, and cause their Faith to enter an era of unprecedented expansion and marvellous and fruitful development. ..."

On 26th June, 1947 came the following cable from the Guardian:

ACCLAIM NEW PLAN CONCEIVED AUSTRALIAN NEW ZEALAND BAHÁ'Í COMMUNITY STOP ADVISE REDUCE PERIOD TO SIX YEARS IN ORDER TERMINATION COINCIDE ONE HUNDREDTH ANNIVERSARY BIRTH BAHAULLAHS PROPHETIC MISSION STOP APPEAL BOTH COMMUNITIES ARISE UNITEDLY DETERMINEDLY ENSURE SUCCESS PLAN MARKING OPENING NEW EPIC DEVELOPMENT FAITH BAHAULLAH ANTIPODES STOP PRAYING ARDENTLY CONSUMMATION DEAREST HOPES STOP CABLING FIVE HUNDRED POUNDS MY CONTRIBUTION PROMOTION PLAN DEEPEST LOVING GRATITUDE SHOGHI

And further on 22nd July, 1947

Dear and valued co-workers:

The Plan, on which the National elected representatives of the Bahá'í communities of Australia and New Zealand have spontaneously embarked marks a turning-point, of great spiritual significance, in the evolution of the Faith in those far-off lands, and is an evidence of the truly remarkable spirit that animates them as well as the communities they represent. I welcome this mighty step they have taken with joy, pride and gratitude, and have hastened to transmit to them my contribution as a token of my keen appreciation of their high endeavours, of my confidence in their ability, and of my admiration for their zeal and noble determination in the service of the Faith. The attention of the members of both communities must henceforth be focused on the Plan, its progress, its requirements, its significance and immediate objectives. All must participate without exception without reserve, without delay. The Administrative Order which they have laboured to establish must henceforth, through its organs and agencies be utilized for the promotion of this vital purpose, this supreme end. For no other purpose was it created. That it may serve this end, that the Plan may speedily develop and yield its destined fruit and demonstrate through its consummation the worthiness, the capacity and high-mindedness of the organized body of the followers of Bahá'u'lláh in those distant lands are the objects of my fervent and constant prayers at the Holy Shrines.

Your true and grateful brother,
Shoghi

Foreword

Many Bahá'í friends have been interested in Jim's meetings with the Beloved Guardian during World War II and on occasions, before Jim passed on to the Abhá Kingdom in 1992, they would ask him to recount his experience. Thus follows his own written account.

The story of how it came about always impressed me because it reveals certain characteristics of Jim: Such as his far-sightedness, his determination and his own love of the Faith.

On returning to Sydney, Australia, in 1941 from Davenport, USA, where he had studied and graduated in chiropractic at the Palmer Chiropractic College, Jim faced the possibility of being drafted in the Army because World War II was in progress. If drafted, he could end up anywhere but because volunteers had a choice of field of service Jim volunteered for the Australian Army Medical Corps, destined for the Middle East where he hoped for the opportunity of meeting the Guardian and visiting the Shrines.

I believe Jim was aware that he could have avoided the draft or volunteering by obtaining employment in a chiropractic firm. Although still a young man in his early twenties with a promising profession, his early object, the spirit of the Faith, stirred him to take another path and thus make a divine pilgrimage, God willing.

Before recounting this wonderful and privileged experience, Jim has provided a brief account of his upbringing and a sketch of his early life, a background to his acceptance of the Bahá'í Faith, as a young man, leading him to the special, unique experience of visiting Haifa during World War II and meeting Shoghi Effendi, the Guardian of the Bahá'í Faith.

Merle Heggie

Part one

An Autobiography by James Heggie

I, James Heggie, was born in Newarthill, a suburb of Glasgow, Scotland, on July 20th, 1915. As my father was in the British Army stationed in the Middle East and my mother worked as a cook away from her home, I was brought up in the home of my maternal grandparents, living with them until 1919 when my father returned from Mesopotamia. My first sight of this strange man with a large cavalry moustache must have alarmed me for I recall my first words to him as "You go back to Mesopotamia and I'll take care of my mother"! With my father's return we visited on two occasions my grandparents in Fifeshire, Scotland, and then in the spring of 1920 we three migrated to Canada and lived in Toronto, Ontario, until 1925 when we moved to Windsor, Ontario. It was here that I was able to take an interest in school work and laid a foundation for an increasing love of books. Having completed my primary education, in the latter part of 1928 and early 1929, I visited relatives in New York City, going to high school there.

It was interesting being in New York, but I never wanted to stay in America. Upon my return to Windsor in February 1929 and in the throes of the depression, my parents decided to remove themselves from the city and chose to take up residence in the northern part of Ontario, which was still in the process of being lumbered and quite primitive conditions prevailed. For a teenager it was wonderful with fishing and canoeing in the summer and skiing in the winter. I spent a great deal of time in the woods by myself hunting or fishing or just roaming about. In the winter the cold was intense - often being sixty degrees below zero, with ice four feet thick on the lakes. In those days I never expected to wear a suit of clothes again.

In 1935, my maternal grandmother and youngest aunt, who had migrated from Glasgow to Australia, visited us as part of a world trip and suggested that I visit them in Sydney. And so it was that in the middle of a cold winter I left home and on New Year's Day 1936 found myself in Vancouver, sailing on the RMS "Niagara" bound for Sydney. In those days, to travel intercontinental meant a sea voyage and when one sails for weeks on end at fifteen knots it imparts an appreciation of the size of our terrestrial globe in a way that air travel never could do.

Calling in at Honolulu briefly after an extremely stormy trip from Vancouver, we touched in at Suva, Fiji and then Auckland, New Zealand and reached Sydney on Australia Day, where I disembarked to launch myself to a life such as I'd never anticipated or experienced. Living in Sydney was a far cry from the outdoor life I had left behind and missed very much at first. However, having found new friends and formed new interests I discovered that Sydney was a very pleasant place to live in and through fortuitous circumstances I formed a friendship which led me to the discovery of the Bahá'í Faith which gave me a new direction, answering questions which I never knew I had and an interest which became the pivot of my life. Indeed, it was to lead me to the Brooks family, but more on that later.

Little did I realize in the summer of 1935 when I made the decision to visit relatives in Sydney that two years later I would be led, seemingly by chance, to the door of a new world. In a world not yet out of the great depression and very soon to enter a second great war and with an agnostic outlook, it now seems fortuitous that in 1937 I found myself spiritually bankrupt and open to many temptations in what I now recognize as an

Jim Heggie in Sydney

unconscious search for some sort of answer to the problems of life.

I had actually attended a meeting or two of some weird nature, and was associated with a Christian Scientist when, in July, I found myself in need of the service of an optometrist as I had hurt my eyes through poor working conditions. Luckily for me, Australia's first believer in the Bahá'í Faith was an optometrist and not a brain surgeon or a psychiatrist. So by chance I called in to the George Street shop of Alex Hale, to find Mr O. Whitaker who not only prescribed the necessary spectacles but also attracted me so that I would always call on him to say hello and talk a little, though it meant waiting perhaps an hour or so.

After a few weeks, I was invited to a youth meeting at Mr Whitaker's home where I first heard the word "Bahá'í". The following weekend, when I visited the George Street shop I told Mr Whitaker I was not interested in religion and he said that it didn't matter and that we would talk of other things.

From then on I visited his home twice a week and we would talk of science for he was wonderfully informative so that soon I came to realize that my disbelief was not against religion but against the inadequate church doctrines. Although Bahá'í literature seemed very limited, we had *"The New Era"*, *"Gleanings From the writings of Bahá'u'lláh"*, *"The Hidden Words"*, and *"Some Answered Questions"* and I found myself confirmed in Bahá'í belief long before I met any of the members of the Sydney community, consisting at that time of fifteen members.

I later found that in all of Australia and New Zealand there were fewer than one hundred believers listed and active in the Faith and that while Martha Root had visited South America and Mr and Mrs Bosch had travelled the South Pacific there was otherwise only an individual or group in South Africa, possibly making a hundred believers in the whole of the Southern Hemisphere. Also, Bahá'í visits were few, being that of Martha Root in 1925, Freddie Schoflocker later and then Keith Ransom-Keiler in 1932. A few Sydney Bahá'ís had visited England but British Bahá'ís had not visited Australia, so it seemed that we were very isolated. When 'Abdu'l-Bahá was in London in 1911 *"The Times"* newspaper carried a full front page on His visit to England and this naturally came to Australia bringing the first news of the Faith. We later found that Miss Stevenson in Auckland, Mrs Lamprill in Tasmania and Mr R.J. Stewart of

James Heggie with Oswald Whitaker and his daughter, Margaret about 1937

Brisbane all heard of the Faith through *"The Times"*, though it was not until Mr and Mrs Dunn came to Australia that action took place.

In 1937, there were three Bahá'í youth, Lucy Trueman and Merle Brooks in Adelaide and myself in Sydney though I did not meet them until I returned from Palestine in 1942. In Sydney there were three Bolton children, in Adelaide two Dobbins children and at Booleroo Centre, South Australia, two

Brooks children, all of whom continued in the Faith. Three other children of Bahá'ís did not continue as members.

Late 1938 and early 1939, we were all excited about the coming of Martha Root's visit - her second and she had us all saying the Tablet of Ahmad each day in preparation for her visit. I attended her Sydney lectures and later in August I was the last Australian believer to see her in Honolulu just before she died. In looking through my diaries of those years, I am quite astounded at the number of Bahá'í activities we had, for though few in number, every possible moment was devoted to the Faith. I note that it was in mid 1938 that I first spoke to Violet Hoehnke of the Faith, she being a friend of my family. I, too, was privileged to often visit the Dunns when they lived in Kirribilli when I was able to help Father Dunn sort out his papers, because his sight was nearly gone. He had a trunk full of typed Tablets from 'Abdu'l-Bahá, as whenever He wrote to the friends in the West the Tablets were copied and spread around among the believers. The Suriy-i-Haykal was one of Father's favourite Tablets.

Much of what I learned of Father Dunn was through Mr. Whitaker. It is interesting to note that though so few in numbers, the believers did not feel overawed by the task of spreading the Faith. They had great conviction as to the power of, and the ultimate success of the teaching work. They were few but they were not weak.

One of the Sydney Bahá'ís was a chiropractor and, upon asking what it was all about, I was told that it was a "A philosophy, science and art of things natural; a system of adjusting the segments of the spinal column by hand only for the correction of the cause of the disease". This I found immediately intriguing and decided to do the necessary studies and follow this profession, which, through the help and encouragement of my aunt I was able to arrange. This required that I travel to America and study at Davenport, Iowa. So it was that I launched myself upon my chiropractic studies when the world launched itself upon the Second World War.

It was at this time that I, all unknown, made my first contact with the Gum or Brooks family, for while on route to the United States and calling in at Honolulu, I visited a friend, bedridden and dying of cancer, who gave me a volume of the *"Bahá'í World"* which contained an article on *Rockwood*

Martha Root's visit to Australia

Father and Mother Dunn

the home of the Brooks family at Booleroo Centre, South Australia and a picture of the home with Merle and Margaret taken in the garden.

My first contact with Bahá'í youth was upon reaching Vancouver on my way to study in America, where I was able to meet the Bahá'í community. My place of study was two hundred miles from Wilmette, which I was able to visit on two occasions. The 1940 Convention was a highlight in my life, for there I met many of the early American believers as well as scores of young Bahá'ís. While in Iowa studying, a number of young Bahá'ís called in to see me while passing through, but the occasions I treasure most were the monthly visits of Mrs. Gertrude Struven who would give a talk at the monthly meetings, which I was able to arrange for, as the N.T.C. was trying to establish an L.S.A. in Davenport. It was Mrs. Struven who introduced me to the study of the Qur'án which was to take up so much of my time in later years. She was an editor of the *"Star of the West"* for many years and was very knowledgable in the Faith and furthered my Bahá'í education with great fidelity. I once dared to question something she said! But only once! Days well spent and remembered.

Upon my graduation as a chiropractor, I briefly visited my family in Canada and then returned to Australia on the *"Aorangi"*. It was on a visit to Brisbane immediately after my arrival in Sydney in May 1941 that I met Hilda Brooks who was there on Bahá'í affairs as she was then the National Secretary.

James Heggie in 1936

James Heggie in 1937

James Heggie in 1941

James Heggie in New Guinea during
WWII March 1945

Jim in army uniform

Part Two

James Heggie's first visit to the Bahá'í World Centre and meeting the Beloved Guardian in December 1941

In the first paragraph of this account Jim refers to his early life, some details of which he also set out in his brief autobiography in Part I that precedes his account of visiting Haifa. Readers may note a little repetition but the editor has not wished to alter or delete any of Jim's narration.

My visits to Haifa in December 1941 and January 1942:

I had not reached my fifth birthday when my parents migrated to Canada, where I spent the next fifteen years, spending my teens mostly in the woods of northern Ontario. In 1935 my maternal grandmother and an aunt visited us while on a world trip and invited me to visit them in Australia, which I reached in January 1936. Of course in hindsight the hand of fate can be readily seen. Perhaps I should say here that I came from a Scottish background, had neither religious leanings nor training and by seventeen had embarked on an agnostic wondering as to the values of this materialistic age.

Sydney, Australia was really an interesting city, but I did miss the open spaces I'd enjoyed in Canada and I was not in love with cities. Thus, by July 1937 I was ready for a change it seems, firstly I'd met a sophisticated gentleman who spoke to me of ideas along the lines of Christian Science and Theosophy etc. and I'd attended one very queer meeting, then my Canadian sweetheart wrote saying she was about to marry the person of her choice, and my work of the moment had brought me a pair of very painful eyes (flashes of electric welding and other stress) so that while I didn't like the idea of wearing spectacles I felt I'd have to do something about it, to wit - I visited an optometrist in George Street, Sydney, who prescribed glasses for me as a temporary measure. I found him a very interesting character and visited him often for several months just to talk to him. He was Mr. O. Whitaker, Australia's first believer in the Bahá'í Faith, who had a very keen scientific mind. So, together we explored a new universe. Thus, when I went to the U.S.A. to study chiropractic, it was as a confirmed Bahá'í and I was able to visit the friends in several cities and to visit the Temple on two occasions. At Convention 1940, I was privileged to meet many of the outstanding believers in North America. One of whom, Mrs. G Struven, introduced me to what became a labour of love which has persisted to this day - the study of the Qur'án.

Very shortly after returning to Australia in April 1941, I volunteered for service in the medical corps in the Australian Imperial Forces and after a period of training again volunteered for a reinforcement draft to the Middle East, where we arrived on November 22nd and were stationed at Gaza. I asked at once to have my leave in Haifa, rather than the flesh pots of Alexandria or Jerusalem where most of the troops took their leave, which was due after a month in camp. So, three days before Christmas, after a late and wet start, we reached Haifa late in the afternoon. I was accompanied by a close friend and we had three days leave to Haifa. As it was getting close to darkness we hurriedly located our previously arranged quarters, in the lower town before turning our faces Carmel-wards in search of the Bahá'í Shrines, where I hoped to discover the whereabouts of the Bahá'ís.

Though in a strange city, the numerous photographs I'd seen of the Bahá'í sites on Mount Carmel allowed us to quickly orientate ourselves, so that having a mental view of the dark cedar-lined gardens of the tomb of the Báb and of 'Abdu'l-Bahá, we made our way up the slope of the mountain, having in the meantime asked in vain for information as to the location of the gardens or of the Bahá'ís. At the upper end of Carmel Avenue, which runs from the harbour and bisects the German quarter, one comes to the long tree-lined stairway, which rises in terraces to the Shrine far above. The ascent is long and tiring, especially when one is so eager to reach the top, yet possibly this is the most suitable approach to the Shrine as one is practically upon one's knees in getting there. The garden is beautifully laid out, the Tomb itself being recessed slightly into the steep slope behind, and terraced on the side facing the Bay of Acca; thus one enjoys a bird's eye view of the city below,

Shrine of the Báb and the surrounding gardens (an early photograph)

The Monument of the Greatest Holy Leaf (an early photograph)

giving way to the artificial harbour and the wide sweep of the Mediterranean with the concave shore on the right hand leading to the ten miles distant fortress of Acca shining whitely in the distance. Haifa is said to be the most beautiful city in Palestine and one can well imagine the Bahá'í gardens there to be a fitting jewel upon the diadem of Carmel. Looking about us upon reaching the Shrine of the Báb we found only two or three gardeners, who, like ourselves were handicapped with but one language, our mother tongue, and who could tell us nothing, while our visit to the nearby establishment offered only the distressing information that the people associated with what she termed the "Persian Gardens" lived in Acca. However, knowing that the Shrines of the family of the Master were nearby, we made our way a short distance down the main motor road which winds its way, from the lower town on its way up the mountain, finding the expected Shrines as seen in the Bahá'í publications.

At first sight, this garden appeared deserted, but in approaching closer we saw a group of men working in the far corner near a building which we later found to be the new archives building; the gates to this garden were shut and being anxious for information I quickly climbed over the wall and approached a rather distinguished gentleman who, dressed in a long coat and wearing a red fez peculiar to the country, was pacing the garden and who having noted the unwarranted entry and determined approach of two uniformed figures, awaited my approach, I, having gone ahead of my companion at this juncture. Upon being asked the whereabouts of the Bahá'ís and saying that I would like to meet them, he told me that all but the "family" had left Haifa and that meetings were no longer held. Feeling very frustrated by this time and reluctant to make myself known as a Bahá'í to a stranger, I was compelled to show him my letter of introduction from the Sydney Assembly which he read, and having done so, warmly welcomed me. Upon expressing my desire to meet the Guardian, the gentleman whose name I did not know, said that he would see us at 9 a.m. the following day, but as I desired to see Shoghi Effendi, I repeated my request and received the same answer, "I will see you at 9 a.m. in the morning", and then calling to a young man who had been a witness to the discussion, said we could visit the Tomb of the Báb and then be shown where to go the following morning.

As there was little time before night set in and the city completely blacked-out, we briefly visited the Tomb of the Báb and looked through the archives in

CONTENTS

Foreword 93

Part One:
An Autobiography by James Heggie ....95 - 103

Part Two:
James Heggie's first visit to the Bahá'í World Centre and meeting the Beloved Guardian December 1941 ....105 -117

Part Three:
James Heggie's second visit to the Bahá'í World Centre and meeting the Beloved Guardian January 1942 ....119 - 123

Part Four:
Quotes in letters from the Beloved Guardian regarding James Heggie ....125 - 127

The gate of the House of 'Abdu'l-Bahá in Haifa

the same building and afterwards made our way to the lower town where we were shown the house of 'Abdu'l-Bahá, as attested by the brass name plate on the wall at the gate, where we were to come the following morning. Our first day of leave ended in having our supper in the Muslim quarter of a blacked-out city in a small cafe where a friendly Greek soldier from a mountain battery offered to share his bottle of a clear liquid from which slowly emerged a bluish vapour!! The following morning we were awakened in our quarters by a young person offering the traditional Middle Eastern glass of red hot black tea, a glass without a handle.

Nine o'clock found us at the house of 'Abdu'l-Bahá where we were admitted by an elderly Persian lady and taken to a sitting-room on the left of the entrance where we were told the Guardian interviewed the pilgrims and where shortly afterwards we were joined by Amatu'l-Bahá Rúhíyyih Khánum, who made herself known to us and informed us that the Guardian would not be long in coming. It was then that I found that the meeting in the garden the previous evening had been with Shoghi Effendi. The Guardian was dressed

The Beloved Guardian Shoghi Effendi

as I'd found him the previous evening, long dust coat and wearing a red fez. I recall his quick smile, his clipped precise speech with the shadow of accent. The Australian Bahá'ís knew so very little of the Guardian - he was to us a revered figure. I now know that whatever one's feelings about Shoghi Effendi prior to and upon meeting him, an hour or two spent in his company is productive of much thought which does not end with one's departure from his presence - for all that is seen and felt in visiting Haifa constitutes a spiritual repast which a lifetime of assimilation is all too short a period to do justice by the task. The Guardian, I've been told since, liked to meet the young pilgrims and talk to them; I can testify to the indelible imprint left by such an experience - one is never the same again.

It would be difficult to say now just what was discussed at that meeting; my friend and I had numerous questions to ask, and the Guardian asked of many of the friends, speaking highly of the efforts of the Bahá'í youth and stressing the greatness of the Cause. It would seem that I was the first western believer the Guardian had seen since his return from England and the first male Bahá'í from Australia to visit Haifa, and thus the many questions he had about the friends in the United States and Australia. He asked particularly about Hyde Dunn whom he had never met in person. This visit was the longest he allowed us and at 11 a.m. he left us, having informed us that we would be taken to Acca and Bahjí that afternoon and that we were to have lunch at the Pilgrim House, to which Rúhíyyih Khánum then escorted us - it being across the street from the Guardian's residence. She told us that she was always pleased to see the pilgrims for she then attended the interviews with the Guardian and heard what he had to say of the Cause, for being so busily engaged with its affairs, the idea of "family chats about the fireside", just didn't exist as such. I was told that the Guardian worked fourteen hours a day having much mail to take care of besides books and tablets investigated, corrected and translated - the occasion in the gardens the previous evening being a period of relaxation which he enjoyed in the quiet of evening, reviewing the work of terracing which was then being carried out, and which my companion and I had so rudely interrupted.

I think it was at this time I asked Rúhíyyih Khánum if it was possible to obtain a Bahá'í ring-stone - so it would be the following day that she surprised me with the Guardian's gift which she brought me, consisting of a Bahá'í ring as well as nine or ten ring-stones and the offer of any Bahá'í book I would like to have (my choice was the newly published Epistle to the Son of the Wolf).

Upon entering the Pilgrim house, we were introduced to Mr. Sutherland Maxwell, who made his home there, and once again met the young gentleman who had been our guide the previous evening, and whom we now found to be Riaz Effendi the Guardian's youngest brother. The following hour I recall was far from sedate, in fact it was a very noisy gathering; so much to discuss, the field of interest so wide and varied, questions of this and that import, besides news to impart of numerous and widely separated Bahá'ís. My friend and I had our first taste of Persian food, finding it a regal banquet, the more so after our stay in the training camps of the Middle East, on tommy rations!

recollections Sketches of Some Early Australian Bahá'ís

A view of the walled city of Akka

Upon the arrival of the taxi, ordered for the afternoon visit to Acca, Riaz Effendi, Jack and myself made our way through the town towards the coastal road leading across the plain of Acca. At the city outskirts, we were halted at a police barrier where the official attitude towards the Bahá'ís was immediately seen; for upon recognizing Riaz Effendi, the officer in charge waved us on our way without interrogation. The plain of Acca was then sparsely built up and its sandy waste stretched the ten miles to Acca, a once trying trip when the only road was a carriage way along the sea shore. At that time I recalled 'Abdu'l-Bahá's description of Haifa and Acca mentioned in the 'New Era' as being ablaze with lights. About half a mile from Acca, Riaz Effendi pointed out to us the Garden of Ridván, a short distance to the right, (the Green Island Bahá'u'lláh has spoken of) almost in the shadow of the hill of Napoleon built by the French army for the placement of the field cannon with which Napoleon bombarded the nut Napoleon could not crack and which he claimed, could he have taken Acca, he would have conquered the East. (It was not for forty years that I found out that the siege guns Napoleon depended upon were captured by Nelson at the Battle of the Nile).

We found the once impregnable and multi-walled fortress in ruins, its harbour now silted beyond use, though the inner walls still remained as evidence of its former greatness. Entering through a gate, low and long, piercing the wall, we found ourselves in Acca much as it was a century and more ago; narrow and dirty streets barely wide enough to allow our vehicle passage - indeed on one occasion upon navigating a turn we took part of the wall with us. In keeping with the tales of Eastern lands, the scene before us was typical of the Arab countries - berobed figures squatting in shops and doorways, tiny overburdened donkeys half-hidden by their enormous loads, dilapidated houses dreary in their grey, square cut, massive build - this was the view which met our eyes as we passed through the city which has attained such importance in Bahá'í history. A picture of neglect and civic decay, yet, until the turn of the century Acca was the chief port of the country, when in 1908 found the release of the Master and the subsequent removal of the Bahá'ís to Mount Carmel and the then small town of Haifa; Acca died, while Haifa boasts a population of 100,000 souls (the locality of Acca, I was then told, claims about 7,000 people, including about 20 Bahá'ís in residence there, who care for the Ridván and the house where the "Family" were domiciled).

Our purpose being to visit the house or apartments occupied by the "Family", we left the car and were escorted to the upper portion by a Persian lady and her son, where we were shown the room used by Bahá'u'lláh which we were told was kept as He left it, though the blinds were drawn and little could be seen other than that it was typical of its day and as shown in the Dawnbreakers. To a Westerner, familiar with modern dwellings built for three or four decades at most, this building which we inspected, ancient in 1870 and with the air of the town in general about it, showed remarkable strength and preservation. We were taken to the more distant portions of the house where we came to the Master's room which being with large windows on three sides offered a magnificent view of Mt. Carmel and the Bay of Acca on one side, with the sea on the West.

Leaving by a gate on the opposite side of the city, we drove about two miles from Acca, gaining a glimpse of the mansion of Bahjí situated by the inevitable olive grove, a short distance from the main road. Here we had to detour around a military area and passed beneath the ancient aqueduct which Bahá'u'lláh caused to be repaired to bring once again a much needed supply of fresh water to the town. Approaching the resting-place of the Blessed Beauty, the mansion was seen to be a two-storied structure and of the same massive nature characteristic of the nearby fortress and of the East in general, partially surrounded by a high wall and with well kept lawns and gardens containing tangerine hedges, tall pine trees and numerous orange trees, many dating from the time of Bahá'u'lláh. Being unable to gain entrance by the huge iron-studded gate, we made our way around to the side where two gardeners were at work, these being brothers belonging to one of the Bahá'í families of Zoroastrian origin remaining to care for the Bahá'í properties - the main community having migrated to Trans-Jordan, where they existed as a farming community.

Upon the instruction of Riaz Effendi, and having greeted my friend and myself, one of the brothers unlocked the door of the Tomb of Bahá'u'lláh while we removed our boots preparatory to entering the Shrine (a wise pilgrim would find slippers very useful in Haifa) and as we stepped within, the gardener greeted us with an expansive smile and a phial of attar of roses, a few drops of which he placed on our hands, which seemed to be a customary procedure. Once inside, I recognized the arrangement of the Shrine as depicted in Bahá'í publications, as one also recognizes the Shrine of the Báb - the vestibule here being roofed with glass and the floor mainly taken up by a small garden with a tree reaching to the ceiling. For me to describe my feelings at such a moment would be quite impossible, for I seemed to be beyond tangible thought, subdued by the overwhelming awareness of the power of the Faith; the outer world appearing extremely remote and unfelt - this feeling I had experienced in the Bahá'í Temple at Wilmette, where within its confines one for a time forgets outside influences. A consciousness of being in a different world, one touching only the spiritual aspect and conveying only a sense of Reality beyond the ability of words to express, for both heart and mind are full: reminding me of the story of a lady visiting Haifa who said to the Guardian, "I don't get this Bahá'í Faith", "No!" said Shoghi Effendi, "but it will get you."

The mansion of Bahjí I found very imposing in its square and massive construction, whatever the lower regions may have been used for in past times they appeared to be quite deserted, only the upper story being occupied; this we reached by an inner stone stairway, narrow and quite steep, leading to a vestibule opening directly into the main hall around which were grouped the rest of the apartments. This central hall, large and airy due to its high ceiling and glass-domed roof took up the centre of the building and with its carpeted floor, mural bedecked walls, gave place to two centre tables upon

The Shrine of Bahá'u'lláh in Bahjí

The Mansion of Bahjí

which were displayed numerous framed documents of note, a model of the Temple at Wilmette and other items of a Bahá'í nature. Several of the rooms leading from the hall were used as libraries, containing shelves of Bahá'í publications, many illuminated tablets, pictures, carpets and the like; before entering these rooms it was again necessary for us to remove our footwear. The apartment belonging to Bahá'u'lláh is situated in the corner closest to Mt. Carmel and is kept exactly as when last used by Him. Here it was that Professor E.G. Browne was privileged to have his memorable interviews with Bahá'u'lláh. Before taking our departure we were offered the small glasses of very hot sweetened tea, beloved of the land, and brought to us in the main sitting room by one of the custodians who had met us in the garden. Here we signed the visitors' book and enjoyed a few quiet moments, parting soon afterwards with our new and ever to be remembered friends at the gate where the taxi had been left and taking with us the tangerines which had been pressed upon us.

Upon returning to Haifa and taking leave of Riaz Effendi, Jack who was a non-Bahá'í was rather surprised that we were not expected to pay for the taxi which, with the driver, had been engaged for the afternoon, for having been to Jerusalem where in visiting the places of Christian interest one is constrained to pay at both entrance and exit and Jack like many others took the situation as usual in Palestine and vicinity; many greatly enthused lads after visiting Jerusalem and surrounding places of historical note, bemoaned the commercialized aspect of the present day and the worldly attitude of the representatives of the various religious establishments. After such experience, one can imagine my companion's conception of Haifa and the Bahá'í world which he had been privileged to contact - where hands are extended in friendship to all who come, in contrast to the grasping figures of those other places; one an empty shell, the other alive and vibrant with life and awareness.

Having but three days leave, travelling included, the following morning found us ready to return to camp and as Jack wanted to have a look around Haifa I was able to spend the morning at the archives with Riaz Effendi. To my great enjoyment, considering three rooms completely filled with historical documents, personal effects of the Báb, Bahá'u'lláh and 'Abdu'l-Bahá as well as innumerable other items of interest, which one would find it difficult to elaborate upon, after such a brief inspection as the morning allowed. Briefly,

An early view of Haifa

recounting as high points I would mention a bust of 'Abdu'l-Bahá, the seals of the Báb, which He sent to Bahá'u'lláh before suffering martyrdom at Tabriz, numerous colourful articles of dress, the writing case of Bahá'u'lláh, as well as that of the Master, a lock or two of Bahá'u'lláh's hair, and the original of the Bayán, many illuminated Tablets beautifully executed, found place throughout the rooms. The one existing photograph of Bahá'u'lláh is, with some colourful paintings of the Báb, displayed on a desk and is quite plainly framed and carefully watched over. Riaz Effendi once again took me to the Shrine of the Báb, where he chanted the Tablet of Visitation, which is printed in tablet form and placed on the wall beside the Shrine. This marked the end of my stay in the World Centre of the Faith, but I left with high hopes of returning to Haifa, leaving with an invitation to stay at the Pilgrim House.

James Heggie

recollections   Sketches of Some Early Australian Bahá'ís

Part Three

James Heggie's Second visit to the Bahá'í World Centre and meeting the Beloved Guardian in January 1942

Some three weeks later, I was once again on my way to visit Haifa. In marked contrast to the first very wet and uncomfortable trip by army truck, the second trip by bus was quite delightful as regards scenery but hair raising from what our Arab driver did with the bus. The weather was beautiful and we passed through numerous orange groves and verdant Jewish settlements, though one must not forget the bullet marked concrete watch towers standing prominently in the groves and settlements. Here and there villages of mud houses peopled by very dirty-seeming inhabitants, small overburdened donkeys and protesting camels were quickly traversed by our madly careering vehicle. The Arab drivers are either the world's best or else fully consigned to the hands of Alláh, and fortunately for us the hand of Fate must have reserved our company for future tasks as we stayed upright and all in one piece to a safe arrival in Haifa.

It was thought provoking to see Arab settlements with their squalid mud huts and antedeluvian methods of farming and life in general, then a few miles away a Jewish community, well laid out, farming on an ultra modern plane and women in all the freedom of western dress; quite a change from the robed and veiled Palestinian Arab women. We had a beautiful view of the sea on our left as we approached Mt. Carmel and could also plainly discern the well-known French monastery perched on the rocky extremity of the mountain as we passed along the narrow strip between the mountain and the sea, soon afterwards entering the outskirts of Haifa with its ultra modern buildings so typical of the Jewish quarters of the larger towns. Situated on the slope of Mt. Carmel the city has a pleasing aspect and brings to mind the description in the "New Era" where 'Abdu'l-Bahá elucidates upon the future greatness and glory of that world metropolis to be. In this visit Haifa smiled;

the white buildings, red-tiled roofs peeping through the greenery of the trees and the sun shining brightly on the shimmering blue of the Mediterranean. We arrived before noon and I at once made my way to Persian Avenue, this time as a guest at the Western Pilgrim House.

The Western Pilgrim House, opposite the home of Shoghi Effendi, is built of stone, as are most residences there, and is of two stories, high-ceiling rooms with barred windows in the lower section. At that time it was very quiet as only Mr. Maxwell lived there, though all but the Guardian had their meals there. The upstairs portion was devoted to the guest rooms and this is where Mr. Maxwell lived. Having settled in, I proceeded to make every minute count by making my way up to the Shrine of the Báb where I found Riaz Effendi supervising the work in the lower garden where I'd first met the Guardian.

This small garden where the Shrines are placed is ideally situated on the road ascending the mountain and so beautifully arranged as to incite the interest of all who pass. The garden rises in terraces with hedge-lined paths, and being winter there, the lawns were a beautiful green, and an avenue lined with cedar trees led from the main gate to the Shrine of the Sister of 'Abdu'l-Bahá, while at the extreme left of the grounds is the new archives building. On our way back to the Pilgrim House we spent some time at the Shrine of the Báb where many of the local inhabitants go to enjoy the peace of the gardens and view the panorama below. Here Riaz Effendi pointed out a small circular grove of conifers above the Shrine of the Báb where it is said Bahá'u'lláh stood with 'Abdu'l-Bahá when He pointed out where the Shrine of the Báb was to be placed. I later found that the grove of similar conifers, where His tent was pitched, is at the bottom of the slope below the Shrine. At one side of the Shrine is located the Eastern Pilgrim House which contains a comprehensive library and which also overlooks the city.

That evening, at dinner, I met another of the Guardian's brothers, Husayn Effendi. These repasts were a delight both in substance and spirit, for there wasn't a dull nor empty moment; I was later taken for a brief visit with the Guardian.

Of the many subjects discussed while in the Guardian's presence two have always remained vividly recalled as we speculated very much on the nature of the universe and of those who peopled its spheres; the other matter concerned the perils of war as regards the ever present possibility of injury and

May the Almighty bless you and sustain you in your devoted labours for the promotion of our beloved Faith, and may He aid you to demonstrate by your life and deeds the vitilizing spirit of our glorious Faith.

(signed) Your true brother,
Shoghi.

18th September 1942 - quote from a letter addressed to Silver Jackman
(Mrs Jackman, (Adelaide) was on the N.S.A. at the time - editor's note)

He was also very happy to hear Jim Heggie has been with you all and is so active in helping the friends all he can and in starting a youth group. He is a very fine young Bahá'í, and the Guardian enjoyed meeting him very much. He hopes in the future many more of the Australian and New-Zealand friends will be able to visit Haifa.

19th March 1943
Quote from a letter addressed to the N.S.A.

P.S. The Guardian replied to Mr Jim Heggie's letter, and he is very pleased to hear of the fine work he is doing. He is also pleased to hear that the work will now go on in connection with Father Dunn's memorial.

30th December 1948
Reference in a letter addressed to the N.S.A.

The letter written by our dear Bahá'í brother, Mr Jim Heggie, as secretary at that time, and dated May 5th, as well as those written by you, etc.

Signed R. Rabbani

22nd March 1949
Cable from the Bahá'í World Centre

Heggie, 47 Ross Street, Fortitude Valley, Brisbane.

LOVING APPRECIATION ARDENTLY PRAYING FORMATION BRISBANE ASSEMBLY the first two years of their confinement in Acca.

Above the door of the room occupied by Bahá'u'lláh was a brass plate giving a brief history of the Faith etc., the authorities having agreed that this section should remain aside from the prison and unused. It was from the roof above that the Purest Branch fell to the floor below, to his martyrdom.

That evening Rúhíyyih Khánum escorted me to the Guardian for the last visit - as I was to leave the next day. We talked for over an hour. I don't remember now what was discussed but the mind still vividly recalls the personality of the Guardian, his voice and mannerisms as he sat in his customary place on a divan just inside the doorway. If only those visits could be repeated, I'm sure I wouldn't talk so much, though I fear he deliberately allowed me full and free expression. I had read all the Guardian's books to that time and was very much aware of his advice and admonition and exposition of the Faith and its values and I know we covered many aspects of Bahá'í importance. Though I did not realize it fully then, my life was to rest on that threshold and my memory of those visits has never faded.

The following morning, having some two hours of freedom left, I visited the new archives where much of interest was displayed. Here I found many books and innumerable tablets. Some time before an eminent Persian calligraphist had spent several months at Haifa illuminating the many Tablets which had been written by Bahá'u'lláh, which the descendants of the recipients of the Tablets had sent them to the Guardian. We saw the Book of Aqdas written in Persian on a large Tablet and many other documents of note. I was very interested to view the sword wielded by Mulla Husayn. As a final item I was able to view the plans for the internal ornamentation of the Temple of Wilmette, fully executed by the architect.

So ends my story. But all that was seen and felt prepared the mind for future elucidation as a ship is victualled for a long voyage. It is afterward that one really sees the Bahá'í World Centre as feelings are weighed and analyzed. One is indeed fortunate in being able to visit Haifa, especially as a Bahá'í, and I often wonder at the hundreds who pass by the Shrines or visit them and how many will afterwards come to appreciate the significance of the Faith of Bahá'u'lláh.

James Heggie in army uniform
about 1943

its aftermath - whether one would be justified in taking one's life if grossly injured, to which the Guardian, after considerable discussion, stated that as long as a person possessed their mental faculties they could fulfil the purpose of life and attain to spiritual enlightenment. The Guardian informed me, as I left his presence, that the following day I was to visit the Barracks at Acca, which being Friday was the weekly visiting day at the State prison where the Persian exiles had spent the first two years in Acca.

The following morning, in the company of Husayn Effendi, I once again visited the mansion of Bahjí, where I was privileged to meet the father of Shoghi Effendi, who at that time lived in the mansion - this was very unexpected as he is little known to us in the west. I found him extremely likeable and interesting. At the same time I was introduced to a Persian Bahá'í who was on his fifth pilgrimage to Haifa with his youngest son, a youth of nineteen years. On his first pilgrimage about 1890 he had met Bahá'u'lláh; the old gentleman was most gracious and though we were unable to converse in English, we exchanged greetings through the Guardian's father.

Upon leaving Bahjí we went to the Ridván Garden which was not far away and off the main road to Acca. It was a very windy day and the noise made it difficult to attract the attention of the custodian of the garden to gain entry. I was shown the small house where Bahá'u'lláh stayed on His visits there; the seat He used is still set among the now much taller pine trees and also the moat which made of the garden Bahá'u'lláh's 'Green Island' which is referred to in the Writings. At one end of the garden was the donkey powered windlass on the well which supplied the irrigation system and moat. The history of the Crusades speaks of a well defined stream of water there. On the opposite side of the roadway is the 'vegetable garden' where the two Bahá'í families who care for the gardens live. They also belong to the community which migrated to Trans-Jordan; I was told that from this community various members of the Bahá'ís pay frequent visits to Haifa bringing some of their produce to the Bahá'ís there.

The hill of Napoleon is very close to the garden. So from the Ridván Garden which is about half a mile from Acca we made our way to the prison gates where we found ourselves fated to cool our heels for nearly two hours in company with a motley array of Palestinians who were visiting the prisoners. Husayn Effendi grew more and more irate as we awaited entry as we had the

The Most Great Prison in 'Akká

necessary authority to visit the rooms used by the Bahá'ís. However it was interesting to study the other visitors while we waited and Husayn Effendi pointed out the windows of the section of the prison where the Bahá'ís were confined and also where Bahá'u'lláh would stand to be seen by the Persian pilgrims who could not gain admittance to the presence of Bahá'u'lláh - a distant glimpse only before departing on their long journey homeward, having but seen Him from without the walls. At last the gates opened and we made our way toward the bridge which gave access to the main building across a dry moat and in company with a Sergeant of Police who was most profuse in his apologies at the delayed entrance, giving some official reason. On passing the guards at the gate of the barracks we found our way to the inside of the prison yet separated from the quadrangle where the inmates conversed with their visitors. Our guide led us by an outside stairway to the upper story of the wing facing the sea where we came to a small though high-ceilinged section from which opened the three rooms where the Bahá'ís spent

recollections   Sketches of Some Early Australian Bahá'ís

Part Four

Quotes in letters from the Beloved Guardian regarding James Heggie

(Quoted from *Messages To The Antipodes* by Shoghi Effendi, Bahá'í Publications Australia 1997)

25th December 1941

Dear Bahá'í brother,

Shoghi Effendi has instructed me to write and thank you for your very kind and generous donation to the Bahá'í Fund here in Haifa. I am enclosing herewith your receipt. He was very happy indeed to meet you, and feels that if you are an example of the Bahá'í youth of Australia, they will render the Cause many valuable services. He wishes to assure you that as long as you happen to be in this part of the world you must consider that you have a home here in Haifa, and any time you can come and visit here you will be most welcome. Also please feel quite free to write him if there is anything he can do for you. Rest assured he will often pray for your protection, and that you may be blessed and guided by God in all things.

With warm Bahá'í greetings,
R. Rabbani

26th December 1941

Quote from a letter addressed to the N.S.A. of Australia.

A few days ago Mr Jim Heggie came to see the Guardian. He was able to visit all the Shrines and archives as well. Shoghi Effendi was delighted with him; he found him devoted, full of faith and zeal, and very well read in the teachings. He feels that if this is a sample of the Bahá'í youth of Australia there is, indeed, a wonderful future ahead of that country!

Signed: R. Rabbani

17th January 1942
Dear Bahá'í Brother,

Enclosed is the receipt for the loving contribution which you insisted on making to the Fund of the Faith here at its World Centre. The Guardian was deeply touched by the motives which prompted you to do this, and he therefore accepts it and will expend it for the Cause here. He was very happy that you were again able to visit the Shrines here, and he assures you that his loving prayers will accompany you, wherever you may be.

With warm Bahá'í greetings,
Yours in His service,
R. Rabbani

15th August 1942
(addressed to Jim) Dear Bahá'í brother,

Your letter of April 12th was received safely, and the Guardian was very happy to see you had gotten back safely to Australia. He has instructed me to answer you on his behalf. It was indeed a great blessing for you that you should have been able, during this world war, to reach the Shores of the Holy Land and make the Bahá'í pilgrimage, even though your time was necessarily short. He hopes some day you will again visit Haifa and spend more time. The difficulties and problems you mention in your letter are ones with which the Guardian is familiar, and he certainly does not mind your mentioning them. On the contrary, he appreciates hearing about them first hand, and is glad you felt free to write to him. This is as it should be.

Signed R. Rabbani

SECTION FOUR

SOME INTERESTING PHOTOGRAPHS

Future Hand of the Cause of God Mr Faizi holding Adrian Heggie with James Heggie holding daughter Jennifer, and daughters of Viva and Jeff Rodwell, standing, circa late 1953 in Brisbane.

James Heggie with Effie Baker at National Bahá'í Headquarters, 1947

*Euphemia Eleanor 'Effie' Baker (March 25, 1880 - January 1, 1968)
Effie became a Bahá'í in 1922 and served for eleven years at
Bahá'í World Centre during the time of the Beloved Guardian*

James Heggie with children: Jennifer at nine, Adrian aged eight and Chris at two years of age

James Heggie delivering a talk

recollections   Sketches of Some Early Australian Bahá'ís

Chris Heggie, Merle Heggie, Amy Brooks, Jennifer Heggie, Adrian Heggie at Gladesville, Sydney 1963

Heggie family 1998
L-R : Chris, Merle, Bita, Sue and Adrian with children Ingrid, Shirin, Stuart

recollections   Sketches of Some Early Australian Bahá'ís

Brooks family gathering at Melbourne Teaching Conference, early 1970s

Back L-R : Geoff Dibdin, David Pepperell, Merle Heggie,
David and Andrew Chittleborough

Front L-R : Colin Duncan, Jennifer Pepperell, Dawn Dibdin,
Adrian Heggie, Marjorie Duncan, Allaine Duncan

recollections Sketches of Some Early Australian Bahá'ís

An early photograph of the National Spiritual Assembly of the Bahá'ís of Australia

(back row from left)
James Heggie, David Hoffman, Joy Vohradsky, Klass Havinga and Stanley P. Bolton.

(front row from left)
Pieter De Vogal, Betty Anderson, John Walker and Joy Stevenson.

(James Heggie went on to be on the National Spiritual Assembly
for many years from 1947, often as Secretary)

1955 National Convention with Effie Baker and Mother Dunn
(Merle Heggie with the children in front row next to Effie Baker)

James and Merle Heggie, Maud Hall, Jean Hutchinson-Smith
and Jane Routh at the first Bahá'í Headquarters

recollections   Sketches of Some Early Australian Bahá'ís

On the steps of the Bahá'í House of Worship, Sydney in late 1960's

Back L-R : Colin Dibdin, Colin Duncan, Geoff Dibdin

Middle L-R : Chris Heggie, Steven Duncan, Merle Heggie, Allaine Duncan, James Chittleborough, Jennifer Heggie

Front L-R : Marjorie Duncan, James Heggie, Dawn Dibdin, Ruth Duncan

First Spiritual Assembly of the Bahá'ís of Burnside South Australia
Hilda Thomas (née Brooks) second from left back row
Ewart Thomas third from left back row

First Spiritual Assembly of the Bahá'ís of Griffith (Wede Shire) 1976
Back row left to right: Nicholas Humphries, Linda Penny, Geoff Dibdin, Kevin Penny, Rod Foster
Front row left to right: Brenda Whitelaw, Dawn Dibdin, Lorraine Sutton, Harry

*The first Spiritual Assembly of the Bahá'ís of Parkes N.S.W. (1968 or 1969)
Left to right back row: Rawdon Middleton, Geoff Dibdin, John Buckmaster, Ted Collis
Left to right front row: Dell Middleton, Jan Peffer, Dawn Dibdin, Enid Buckmaster, Jean Collis*

*Left to right: Madge Painter, Nell Mc Miles, Marjorie Duncan and Merle Heggie
in the grounds of the Sydney Bahá'í House of Worship*

Group outside Heggie Home Gladesville, Sydney 1976
Standing L-R : Adrian and Melanie Heggie, Merle Heggie, James Heggie, Jennifer Pepperell née Heggie, David Pepperell. Front : Chris Heggie

James with his sisters Euphemia and Nancy visiting from Canada and his grand child Shirin in 1991

recollections Sketches of Some Early Australian Bahá'ís

*James and Merle Heggie
with some of the grand children*

James Heggie at Home in Gladesville

James Heggie in the garden at Home in Gladesville

THE FAMILY TREE

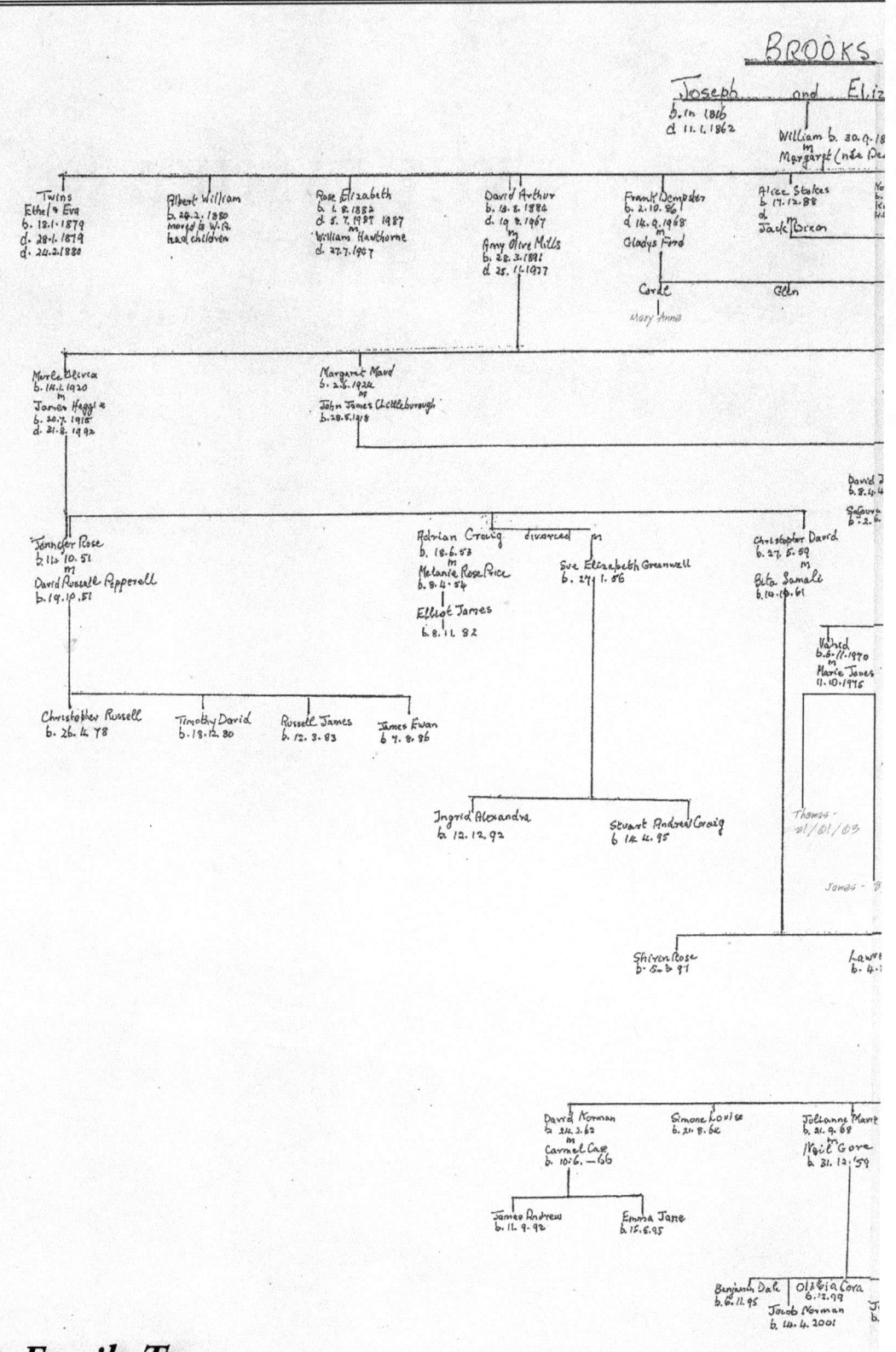

The Family Tree

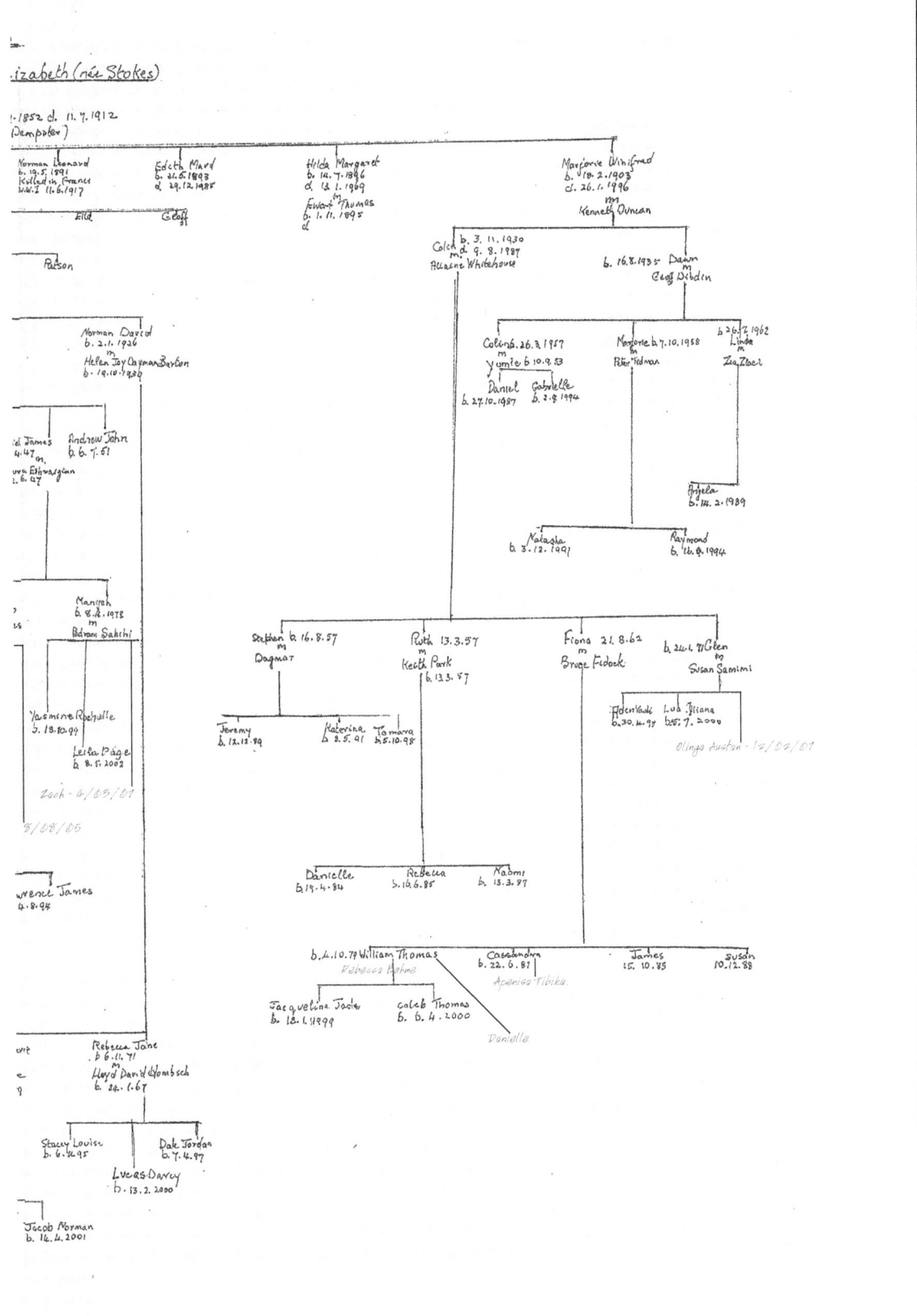

EPILOGUE

With gratitude and happiness I have recorded very briefly the outcome or the effect that the divine message of Bahá'u'lláh had on reaching some people in Australia. It was brought here by travel teachers or pioneers of the Faith during the early nineteen hundreds and resulted in its acceptance by many members of the family. Indeed Baha'i members of the family now span six generations and actively participate in many fields including a Counsellor, the N.S.A., L.S.A., B.R.C., assistants to Auxiliary Board members, and committees, as well as teaching activities such as youth service overseas. Many are prominent in their own professions. Rather than an Epilogue these few words might well be considered as a prologue to the next chapter.

Hand of the Cause of God, Mr. Faizi once commented that he thought the Brooks family to be the largest western Baha'i family. Many factors have helped contribute to this situation including the strength of character required of those early pioneers to a virgin territory, the strong personalities formed strong bonds in their family relationships which in turn led to strong commitment to the new Faith.

Team work was a natural way of life for the members of the family and where members enjoyed the bounty of marriage to another Baha'i the result almost invariably was a new generation only too keen to carry on in and work for the Cause.

One of the most important factors in leading a young Baha'i child to continue in the Faith after attaining the age of maturity at fifteen must be a home life where the sometimes demanding requirements of active involvement in Baha'i administration and teaching are conducted in a spirit of love and joy, a spirit of service to Bahá'u'lláh and humanity. The moment a child feels that their parents religion is taking them away from the family they will begin to resent it, unless they too share desire or vision of the Faith. It is evident that in all cases where one member of the marriage partnership has been required to devote a large proportion of their time to administrative duties, there has been unreserved support from the spouse.

Having been introduced to the Faith by Hands of the Cause of God and been in regular contact with other Hands should not be overlooked as indeed being in communication with the beloved Guardian of the Cause must have strengthened their resolve and determination.

But in the end it comes down to the overwhelming love for Bahá'u'lláh's Cause that exerted its influence on each successive generation and we trust, on generations to come.

FAMILY SURNAMES

Brooks
Chittleborough
Heggie
Duncan
Dibdin
Pepperell
Park
Fidock
Palliaer
Ziai
Tidman
Sahihi

SECTION THREE

James Heggie
(20/7/1915 - 31/8/1992)

And on 30th April, 1949 (National Convention)

ASSURE DELEGATES FRIENDS DEEPEST LOVING APPRECIATION NOBLE SENTIMENTS STOP ARDENTLY PRAYING BEFITTING DISCHARGE SACRED RESPONSIBILITIES STEADY EXTENSION CONTINUED CONSOLIDATION MAGNIFICENT LABOURS AUSTRALIAN NEW ZEALAND BAHAI COMMUNITIES STOP DEEPLY GRATEFUL HISTORIC SERVICES ALREADY RENDERED FAITH BAHAULLAH   SHOGHI

A brief quote from a lengthy letter signed by his secretary, R. Rabbani is as follows:

"22nd August, 1949

The news that there is now a Spiritual Assembly in every capital city of the various states in Australia pleased him immensely. This is an historic land-mark in your progress out there, and must act as a keen incentive to further exploits on the part of the Australian Bahá'ís."

Thus, step by step, little by little, the beloved Guardian's inspiring messages urged and guided us on.

On first appearance Brisbane seemed a "tacky city". The war years had seen little or no progress. Finding accommodation was difficult. However we were lucky in this respect. Thanks to my Aunts, temporary accommodation was arranged: an interested contact at one of their public meetings suggested to them that her neighbour could offer us accommodation, so they arranged it before we left Sydney.

On alighting from the taxi with our few items of luggage displayed on the footpath, the landlady, there and then, raised our previously agreed-upon rent. Although we had very few possessions at the time and no jobs of course, it was a disconcerting welcome on arrival.

It was an experience living in that small weatherboard house after the comfort of the Hazíratu'l-Quds in Sydney. Our kitchen was on the back verandah, very exposed to all the weather; there was no bathroom. Such needs were supplied by an old, round, tin tub to carry hot water from a little back-yard fire to the laundry to wash our linen or to bathe in. A hole in the bedroom wall to peep into the kitchen (or the opposite view) had to be plugged; in retrospect rather amusing but not then. After a few weeks there we found better accommodation.

When we arrived in Brisbane there were in that city three Bahá'ís: Mr. Jack Bedgood, his mother, Mrs. Bedgood and a Mr. Stewart, a dentist whose first name I cannot recall. Our first task was to seek these three souls in Brisbane. We made quick contact with them. Jack Bedgood and his mother, Mrs. Bedgood, welcomed us in their home. We knew Mrs. Bedgood's sister in Sydney, both of them Bahá'ís. Then we met Mr. Stewart who had first learnt of the Faith reading a London newspaper article that made reference to 'Abdu'l-Bahá's visit to the British Isles. About this interesting early contact with the Faith I recall no further details - Alas!

Jim found rooms in which to set up practice as a chiropractor and, for a time as well, he worked at night in a factory travelling to and from on his motor scooter. The manager of this factory and his wife, Frank and Dorothy Farley, became Bahá'ís.

I had a job first as a typist in a car firm, then in the Australian Broadcasting Commission, as an assistant, preparing or checking scripts, interviewing professors, lecturers, curators and various people in work or activities that would interest or inform children. These people would usually participate in the "Broadcast to Schools" programmes. I prepared the material briefly for the school booklet. It was an interesting job. I was encouraged by the head of that department to apply for an assistant's job involving the actual production of school broadcasts which I think would have been rewarding and interesting, but because I had just become pregnant I declined applying, thinking that it would be too much of a challenge during my first pregnancy. Two of my children were born in Brisbane.

There were several declarations and by 1949 an L.S.A. was elected, members of that Local Assembly being as follows:

mission entrusted to the care of the Faith in Australia and New Zealand is by no means confined to the mainland of Australia and the islands of New Zealand, but should embrace, as it unfolds, in the years to come, the islands of the Antipodes, where the banner of the Faith still remains to be unfurled and its Message is as yet undelivered.

And on 13th August, 1948 to the National Spiritual Assembly

DELIGHTED PROGRESS ACHIEVE URGE CONCENTRATE IMMEDIATE EFFORTS FORMATION ASSEMBLIES BRISBANE PERTH ALL SAFE LOVING APPRECIATION SHOGHI

Then on 22nd March, 1949

Heggie 47 Ross Street, Fortitude Valley, Brisbane.

LOVING APPRECIATION ARDENTLY PRAYING FORMATION BRISBANE ASSEMBLY

And again 1st April, 1949 (National Spiritual Assembly)

CABLE NUMBER ASSEMBLIES GROUPS ISOLATED BELIEVERS AUSTRALIA NEW ZEALAND ALSO NUMBER EXPECTED ASSEMBLIES COMING RIDVAN - SHOGHI RABBANI

And 22nd April, 1949

Brisbane Bahá'ís, care Natbahai, Sydney:

APPRECIATE GREETINGS REJOICE ELECTION ASSEMBLY LOVING REMEMBRANCE SHRINES

And 22nd April, 1949

Perth Bahá'ís, 88 Thomas Street, West Perth.
DELIGHTED ASSURE YOU PRAYERS HEARTFELT CONGRATULATIONS.

Then on 6th December, 1947 (National Spiritual Assembly)

OVERJOYED GLORIOUS NEWS MAGNIFICENT PLAN ALL IMPORTANT TEACHING WORK DEEPEST ADMIRATION EXEMPLARY SPIRIT CABLING FIVE HUNDRED POUNDS MY CONTRIBUTION REALISATION NOBLE PURPOSE ARDENTLY PRAYING SUCCESS DEEPEST LOVE SHOGHI

And on 4th May, 1948 to the National Spiritual Assembly

NATIONAL SYDNEY

ASSURE DELEGATES LOVING FERVENT PRAYERS SUCCESS DELIBERATIONS FULFILLMENT HOPES URGE PERSEVERANCE ENSURE VICTORIOUS CONCLUSION PLAN SHOGHI

And on 11th May, 1948:

Dear and valued co-workers,

The Plan launched by the small yet highly promising community of devoted believers in Australia and New Zealand constitutes a landmark of unusual significance in the history of the evolution of the Faith in that far-off continent. It opens a new chapter, rich in promise, momentous in the events which it must record, and destined to be regarded as a prelude to still more glorious chapters in the annals of the Faith in the Antipodes.

The limited resources at the disposal of the prosecutors of the Plan, the vastness of the territory in which it must operate, the fewness of the numbers of those participating in its execution, offer a mighty challenge which no loyal follower of the Faith of Bahá'u'lláh can either ignore or minimize. Indeed the greater the challenge, the more bountiful the blessings which will be vouchsafed from on high, and the richer the reward to be won by its triumphant executors.

The successful termination of this Plan, the first fruit of the newly established and properly functioning Administrative Order in those distant lands, will pave the way for the launching of still greater enterprises, destined to carry the message of Bahá'u'lláh to the Islands of the Pacific in the vicinity of that continent. For the

Once when working on it and keeping an eye on his lively three-year old daughter, he was distracted and had an accident, nearly severing the top joint of his finger; later he jokingly referred to his shedding of blood for the Faith. Jim had a dry sense of humor. He even worked out a Bahá'í Calendar. As far as I can remember, the Guardian commended his effort. Alas! I cannot find it now.

We found Queensland people very friendly and hospitable. Our community grew, at first through personal contacts and the help of travel teachers. Then later public lectures were arranged. Very memorable and comforting was the visit of the Hand of the Cause of God, Mr. Furutan and Mr. Faizi (the latter not a Hand at the time). I'll never forget the impact of their presence: their love, encouragement and percipience. There was a radio interview arranged for them that I found very disappointing, the reason being due to my inexperience. For some reason, surely not the usual policy of that radio station, the job of the interviewer was, on the spot, allotted to me. I wasn't forewarned and I was inexperienced and certainly not prepared for the task. I was mortified. Nevertheless, Hand of the Cause spoke of the Faith and enlightening statements must have been broadcast.

In the late summer of 1954 when Jim again became secretary of the N.S.A. we returned to Sydney, confident in the devotion of the Brisbane friends to the Faith and their ability to establish a sound and expanding community.

Years later, passing through Brisbane we found a thriving, modern city in a new garb with lovely aspects, new buildings, splendid gardens and best of all, a large, energetic and devoted Bahá'í community.

recollections   Sketches of Some Early Australian Bahá'ís

Mr. Jack Bedgood	*Chairman*	Miss Lilian Bridge
Mr. Frank Farley	*Vice Chairman*	Mrs. Dorothy Farley
Mr. James Heggie	*Secretary*	Mrs. Gertrude Squelch
Mrs. Merle Heggie	*Treasurer*	Miss Marjorie Squelch
Mrs. Bedgood Snr.		

Mention must be made concerning the visit of Joseph Perdu to Brisbane where he stayed several weeks, perhaps a few months. Jim and I were delighted to meet him. He was very knowledgeable and an experienced Bahá'í. He could give an interesting public talk, he made friends easily and invited them to meetings; he was very persuasive as a teacher of the Faith and Jim and I adopted him like a brother in our new and rather lonely surroundings. He gave Jim a few lessons in Persian. He taught us a Persian recipe, perhaps it was Indian being very spicy. Jim and I made it many times.

It was a very sad awakening to the knowledge that Joseph was not all he seemed. I began to query to myself his far-fetched claims about his meetings with world-renowned people and other questionable remarks that he made at times. He foolishly gave me a letter in French, addressed to him, that I was able to read, much to his surprise and seeming dismay, as it read like a love letter. Joseph knew his ways and actions as a Bahá'í were becoming known and questioned. About that time he likened himself to a plane about to crash.

In due course the N.S.A. warned us about his activities. It was a shock to us and to many of the new Bahá'í friends and for a short time some of the friends did not attend a few meetings. One member, Lilian Bridge, we never saw again, nor were we able to contact her. However, we quickly recovered to become again an active, happy community.

While in Brisbane for those five and a half years, Jim was always busy with Bahá'í projects such as learning Braille and then transcribing some of the Teachings into Braille (using the old method) and presenting the books to the Blind Society. He also printed Bahá'í material with a hand-operated printing machine and then a foot-operated system. With this latter machine he printed pamphlets that had been translated from English to a language of the Pacific. This latter machine he installed under the house.